HOW TO LOOK AT DANCE

Other Books by Walter Terry

HOW TO LOOK
AT DANCE

WALTER TERRY

with photographs by
Jack & Linda Vartoogian

Designed by Judith Adel

William Morrow and Company, Inc.
New York   1982

Library of Congress Cataloging in Publication Data

Terry, Walter.
   How to look at dance.

   Bibliography: p.
   Includes index.
   1. Dancing. I. Vartoogian, Jack. II. Title.
GV1595.T43   793.3   81-14111
ISBN 0-688-00777-5   AACR2

Printed in the United States of America

First Edition

1 2 3 4 5 6 7 8 9 10

For Foster Fitz-Simons. If Foster had not said to me when we were college teenagers, "A Mrs. Barr has started some dance classes on campus—shall we give it a try?" I might never have written this book nor, indeed, the twenty other books on dance and dancers that have preceded it. So to Foster—dancer, choreographer, teacher, director, poet, schoolmate and lifelong friend—thank you for exploring *How to Look at Dance* with me.

Acknowledgments

Special, as well as initial, thanks to Linda and Jack Vartoogian for their patience and diligence in delving into their vast files of contact sheets and even negatives in search of the exact illustrative material I needed for every step, stance, style, for every gesture and nuance. My gratitude to David Manion, director of the Riverside Dance Festival, for permitting us to photograph at his facilities, and to Rebecca Wright and George de la Peña, splendid and versatile artists of the dance, for executing the special movements I asked for while Jack shot the pictures. I owe undying gratitude to Ivan Nagy, one of the great dancers of this era, for not only listening sympathetically to my theories and studies contained in the chapter on "The Meanings of Movement," but also for testing them with enthusiasm to successful conclusions. My gratitude also to Stuart Sebastian, choreographer and teacher, for his help in exploring these same areas of meaningful movement under rehearsal and classroom conditions. And could I ever write a book containing ethnic-dance material without consulting La Meri? Certainly not!

Contents

Movements from *The Afternoon of a Faun*—Rudolf Nureyev and Charlene Gehm, Joffrey Ballet.

Athletes

We are living in a Golden Age of Dance. As we sit in the theater or before our television sets, Mikhail Baryshnikov in tremendous leaps soars past our eyes. Rudolf Nureyev, ballet's superstar, dressed as a golden faun, presses his loins against a scarf dropped by a nymph who has escaped his sensual embrace. A ballerina, ineffably light, floats into view. From a jazz chorus in a musical show, on stage or on TV, a single figure explodes into space, a human rocket from a choreographic launching pad. These moments make us gasp in wonder at the prowess of the human body in action. It's the Olympics set to music! Exciting in the extreme, *but,* as Peggy Lee has sung so plaintively, "Is that all there is?" No. There is more, much more, if we know what to look for.

The parallel of the dancer and the athlete is the best starting point for the voyage of discovery into the world of dance. Martha Graham, in her eighties the dowager empress of America's modern dance, has referred to dancers as "divine athletes." To give action to her words, she created her long-popular work for full company of men and women, *Acrobats of God* (1960). Theologians may quite properly debate whether dancers are "divine" and whether God looks upon them as His "acrobats." But dancers, physically and aesthetically, do bring an extra dimension to the stance and the stamina, the strength and the shape, the movements and the very prowess of the basic athlete.

Lynn Swann, the great wide receiver of the Pittsburgh Steelers, started out as a dancer. His mother sent him to dancing school—jazz and tap—for fourteen years. Yet by the sixth grade of elementary school in San Mateo, California, he was already a team member in the field of sports.

"Some of our greatest athletes might well have become some of our greatest dancers if prejudice against dancing for men had not stood in the way," says Swann. "One can always see the presence of dance in sports. Both require endurance, agility, balance, strength and body controls of all kinds. In sports the good athlete must know that if he needs to leap or jump, that the leap is *for* a specific purpose, that you are leaping *at* or leaping *away* from something. In ballet you learn that the *landing* from this leap is the *beginning* of a move in a new direction. Athletes can use this."

The dancer's body—Rudolf Nureyev
in Paul Taylor's *Aureole*.

Grand jeté—Mikhail Baryshnikov
in *Theme and Variations*.

Swann, who is on the board of directors of the Pittsburgh Ballet
Theater, not only does TV commercials for this important ballet
company but also practices ballet. Swann explains, "In Pittsburgh,
and in any big city, we need culture as well as industry, art as well as
sports. By my being on the ballet's board, I'm acting as a bridge
between the fans of our team and the fans of the ballet. And by doing
this, I hope all of them will discover the similarities between two
great activities."

The late, great Ted Shawn (1891–1972) long recognized the link
between sports and dance and found in it a way to dispel America's

Grand jeté—
Natalia Makarova
rehearsing
Don Quixote.

prejudice against any male dancer other than the show-biz hoofer. His career as a concert dancer had begun in 1911 and continued from 1915 to 1931 with his wife and partner, Ruth St. Denis. Their fabulous Denishawn era saw their companies performing around the world. But although Shawn created and performed virile dances of primitive and classical warriors during this period, it was not until he formed his all-male company in 1933 that he determined to proselytize the art of dancing through athletics.

For his pioneering venture, he selected as dancers young men who were proven athletes, most of them with college letters in

sports. The group included a youth who held an intramural collegiate boxing championship, another who had made a pole-vault record and others who had excelled in wrestling, fencing, basketball, decathlon and so on. In 1936 Shawn created for them *Olympiad,* a big dance number based on the sports in which they excelled. It was a huge hit with audiences, but the blockbuster dance was the opening solo, "The Banner Bearer." Here, a dancer with a long pennant attached to a pole raced on stage to announce the "games" as the runner had done in the days of ancient Greece. As the dance reached its climax, he made his body spin within an

The Faun—George de la Peña—rehearsing movements from
Nijinsky's *The Afternoon of a Faun*.

orbit described by the swirling banner. While he bore the banner in a great circle around the stage, he executed high, arching leaps within the arcs etched by the streaming banner.

In Shawn's *Olympiad* and in Gerald Arpino's *Olympics* (another all-male dance created thirty years later for the Joffrey Ballet), it was not necessary to tell the laymen in the ballet audiences what to look for. It was all there, that relationship between sports and dance that Lynn Swann talks about today, fifty years after Ted Shawn began to plan for a company of "dancing athletes." But there were differences between *Olympiad* and *Olympics*. The Shawn work was much more literal in its relating of a sport to its dance extension than was Arpino's more subtle, sophisticated treatment.

In the Shawn dance, the element of pantomime was strong. Everyone understands pantomime—often it is the appropriate gesture, long familiar to everyone, without the prop. Thus the dancing fencers, moving to music, thrust and parried; the boxer, struck by an unseen opponent, ricocheted against imaginary ropes; the wrestlers in hammerlocks pulled each other's hair and let out soundless yelps; and the Olympic runner, without any hurdles on the track, leaped over his own extended leg. With Arpino's choreography, various sports and skills were not so much reproduced in choreographic shape as they were distilled into studies of speed, lightness, resilience, strength. Still, the essence, if not the acts, of the Olympic Games was present.

The sportsminded newcomer to the art of dancing would have no trouble understanding and relishing *Olympiad*. The viewer might even concede, "Gee, I wish our team players were as fast and light on their feet as those dancers." With *Olympics* an audience would have to look a little more closely. That run with quick shifts in direction—is that basketball or football? That place where they come at each other hard, that's got to be a scrimmage. A little guesswork here, but that too is part of the game.

Lynn Swann, in his boyhood, was mastering a dance technique that required little explanation. Tap dancing can be complex— rhythmically—but rarely is it complicated. Dexterity, in the athletic sense, is present, so the tap dancer is also an athlete. But it is hardly necessary to describe the best way to *look* at tap dancing, for it is just as important to *listen*. The tap-dance expert uses toe, heel and full foot to create a vast array of rhythmic patterns that fascinate the ear, but the tapster, aware of the visual side of his skills, attempts to make those steps fun or exciting to see: swift changes of the beat from one foot to the other; traveling patterns in circles or straight lines; hops and jumps and slides; forward leans and backward runs; perhaps splits or a batch of ballet's *pirouettes*. Sound and sight go together here in tap. For a sports star like Lynn Swann, the connecting link between the early studies of tap and the later involvement with ballet was . . . sports itself.

For the dance novice, ballets based on sports to dances that have nothing whatever to do with sports may seem a giant step. But it is not. In the classical ballets about princes and princesses, heroes and

Nureyev in *The Afternoon of a Faun* (Joffrey Ballet).

villains, there are splendid moments when athleticism—not athletics—prevails. Here are the moments when, say, Baryshnikov launches himself into space, spins in air and lands in a spectacular lunge. The crude equivalent may be discerned in those tense and near-violent seconds that may determine the outcome of a football game. As Lynn Swann points out, "What we do as athletes is related to choreographed action, but the difference lies in the fact that while the dancers are held to the discipline of the choreography itself, we, in the progress of the game, must use our discipline in the not-always-anticipated movements of the game itself."

It is not surprising that a Golden Age of Dance should arise in the 1970s and 1980s when the Olympic Games have assumed new political as well as athletic importance. Today entire families are glued to TV sets during baseball and football seasons, bowl games, the Winter Olympics, tennis matches and golf tournaments. When dancers appear on television, as they do in increasing numbers and on ever more frequent occasions, viewers may quite logically look for an equivalence with athletics. Yes, there are the superb, muscled bodies of the men; the supple, deceptively strong, graceful movements of the women. As Dad's appreciative eye takes note of a ballerina doing a *grand battement* (the elegant version of a kick), or a modern dancer in a high leg extension, he murmurs, "Boy, she sure can kick high!" This is said with enormous admiration and it is a compliment. But what his eye records is the superficial aspect of a "kick."

The novice newspaper reporter, when sent out on assignment by his (or her) editor, is told that in looking for a story he or she must remember to report on five factors in a news event: the WHO, the WHAT, the WHERE, the HOW, the WHY. The novice dance viewer has not looked to see *how* the dancer kicks, or to discover *why* she kicks, or to think about *where* the kick comes in the choreography or to notice that *when* it comes in the choreography may have something to do with drama, characterization, mood or, simply, pattern.

A high kick by Matt Bahr, a valued kicker with the Pittsburgh Steelers, multiple high kicks by the Radio City Music Hall Rockettes, a floating high kick in Act II of *Giselle* by the ghostly heroine and the stabbing high kick of Jocasta in Martha Graham's *Night Journey* have little in common other than an agreeably (and necessarily) loose pelvis. Each of these kicks, and hundreds more, exist for a different

On ice skates—John Curry in his IceDancing version of
The Afternoon of a Faun with Cathy Foulkes.

purpose. All the viewer need do is look for that purpose. Why
bother? Because pleasures will be increased, emotions stirred and
the horizons of human experience extended.

If this Golden Age of Dance is to survive, if it is to be more than a
passing novelty, those millions of newcomers to dance, by way of
the mass market of television, must look for something more than
prowess, something more than athleticism set to music.

The incredible dance explosion television has helped create has
created responsibilities. These should be shared equally by pro-
ducers and viewers, for if dancing is to be simply the major novelty

Tap dance—Judith Jamison and
Bernard Lias (Off-Broadway show).

16

that the earlier mass medium of communication, radio, could not exploit, then it will not enrich our culture or us to its fullest potential.

Today's dance explosion is a fact. It had its rumbling beginnings more than half a century ago, and by the early 1970s it had swelled to the degree that from 1970 to 1975 attendance at dance events had increased an incredible 600 percent. This percentage represented audience participation in the theater. By 1980 the number of viewers seeing dance programs or interludes on television was almost incalculable.

Parallel to the dance explosion of TV has come the explosion of live dance events on the community level. The regional ballet movement came into being officially twenty-five years ago. Atlanta had a ballet group of modest size and purpose as far back as the 1920s; the San Francisco Ballet began in 1933; other cities commenced to build amateur ballet groups out of the most promising pupils from local ballet schools. But for the most part, the average community settled for (or put up with) the annual dance-school recital in which the harried teacher had to provide at least one step or pose for each of her pupils for the delectation of proud mothers and grandmothers, and the stifled groans of fathers. It didn't much matter what the kids did as long as they were "cute." The art of the dance was far, far away.

With the surge of national interest in ballet and the swift growth of ballet schools and classes in every community, other styles of theatrical dance did not disappear. The smashing success in 1971 of a revival of the 1920s musical comedy *No, No, Nanette* triggered a revival of interest in tap dancing not only for Broadway shows, but also for television and in dance schools across the country. Veteran black tap dancers came out of semi-retirement to perform once again and to show new generations the different steps and styles that were born in Harlem night spots or on old vaudeville circuits. In concert appearances and on TV, these old-timers showed audiences what to look for in the subtleties of the form, from hard, flashy tap to the old soft shoe, from delicate footwork to slides and splits.

Today, with professional dance companies in most of our big cities and a hundred regional advanced amateur, semiprofessional and even professional troupes, the standards of dance instruction, the quality of dancing, the caliber of choreography, and the taste in production have risen to unexpected planes of excellence. Where the old dance-school recital was of interest only to the relatives of the paying pupils, regional performances constitute a cause for community pride.

Nowadays no Christmas season is complete without a local production of *The Nutcracker* ballet. But ballet should not be seasonal. Thus directors of ballet companies from coast to coast entice their audiences with modest productions of *Swan Lake* or *Giselle* or *Coppélia;* but to get viewers to go beyond the increasingly familiar classics with their equally familiar musical accompaniments, they institute subscription series which include, aside from the "bait," new dance works that may be innovative, challenging, even disturbing.

Today's dance explosion has at its core the "ballet boom," and it is the sudden proliferation of ballet events on stages and on screen that has left the viewer with the need for guidelines to assist in getting the most out of dance. This is true whether one is watching the easy-to-follow *Nutcracker* with its familiar music and its promise that Christmas is here, or Antony Tudor's *Dark Elegies,* a ballet based on the mournings for dead children. Modern dance, with its plumbing of psychological motivations for movement behavior or its experiments with dance-by-chance, represents an important part of the "explosion" as do ethnic-dance forms representing the ancient and very special heritages of many distant cultures.

Choreographers, directors and dance artists want the public to journey with them beyond the "gymnastic tricks and pretty movements" that Isadora Duncan decried. For thousands of years, theatergoers have been amused by Aristophanes, frightened by Sophocles and warned by Euripides; they have been entertained by the commedia dell'arte and berated by Ibsen; they have laughed and loved with Shakespeare's *A Midsummer Night's Dream,* yet shivered with the evils of *Macbeth* and pondered their own sanity as Hamlet

Dramatic gesture—
Martine Van Hamel
rehearsing Tudor's
Dark Elegies.

A jump (*sauté*)—Mikhail Baryshnikov with
Marianna Tcherkassky in *The Nutcracker*.

mused on his. Compelling drama is not a barrel of laughs. Compelling dance is not a matter of gymnastic tricks and pretty poses.

It is the purpose of this book to take newcomers to the art and the act of dancing on a journey through the meanings and marvels of movement. There is no reason to lose interest in a dance when an altitudinous leap and a vertiginous spin are completed or when the *premier danseur* has won the endurance record for multiple *entrechats*. See what happens when the strong male hand touches the fair shoulder of the ballerina? Yes, in reflex, she rises onto *pointe*, but she is not going to do any tricks, for the touch, the only touch in the world, has lifted her to a plane of ecstasy. Study the lady in the heavy dress of black and gold as she bends ever so slightly in a falsely servile bow; her body trembles with rage and you know the recipient of that obeisance is going to die at the hand of a Borgia. There stands Jocasta—with a terrible wrench her leg leaves the floor, and, racing higher and higher, it reaches beyond her head and is clutched into agonized place. It is a soundless, enormous cry from the loins, and you know, looking at it, that a monstrous crime has been committed. No, it wasn't just a high kick; it was a statement of towering theater. . . .

2   Steps and Styles of

Balance on *pointe*—Cynthia Gregory in Rose Adagio (*The Sleeping Beauty*) at a gala performance with veteran *danseurs* Igor Youskevitch (back to camera), the late André Eglevsky and Scott Douglas.

Dance

The need to communicate is universal. Our tools for communication are movement and sound. Movement came first. We cannot utter a gurgle, a moan, a hiss, a call, a cry, a yell, a shriek without movement: We inhale to prepare for sound and exhale to make that sound. The raw materials of words are sounds. These words can range from a child's "Daddy" and "Mommy" to Shakespeare's Juliet sigh of "O Romeo, Romeo! wherefore art thou Romeo? . . ." As the range of words and their possible inflections are endless, so too is the range of movement eloquence.

Each of us has mastered a vocabulary of words, as limited or as extensive as our needs or our jobs require. To experience an eloquence of words beyond our own capacities, we go to the theater, look at television or listen to the radio. We may be captivated by the words of a playwright spoken by a great actor with an urgency and a power of which we are not capable. Give a lilt, patterns of pitch, disciplines of rhythm to words and you have song, musical theater, grand opera. Potentially every one of us may strive for the eloquence of the writer, the playwright, the orator, the actor, the singer. Few of us do. So, vicariously, we find our own potentials achieved in the accomplishments of others, of creator-performers.

There is also a vocabulary of movement. Before language evolved, gesture served to warn or inform, or, as in the ageless braggart fisherman's story, "You should have seen the one that got away." With movement, as with speech, most of us settle for a comfortable minimum. We walk and run, stoop and reach, sit and stand; inadvertently we might fall (from slipping or fainting) or jump (from surprise or a hotfoot). We use gesture to indicate "Come here!" or "Over there!" or "Stop!" and we all know several that serve to tell someone off. For movements of a higher physical order, we look to the athlete. For movements transfigured by beauty of execution, incandescent with total body vitality, vibrant with the urgency to action, we look to the dancer.

The dancer must master a vocabulary of movement far more extensive and complex than that sufficient to the ordinary person. Unlike vocabularies of words, which fall into hundreds of tongues and thousands of dialects, vocabularies of movement have one common denominator—the human body. There are two arms, two legs, a trunk, a head and a prescribed number of appendages essential to dance: two feet, two hands. The Hindu temple dancer may move quite differently from the ballerina, but the same number of parts are involved—no more, no less. A Hindu dance elbow and a balletic elbow can move in only one direction; this limitation is common to all humans. The shoulder is rotary, enabling the arm to move in all directions—this potential is common to all humans. When we come to look at dancing, we are faced with a familiar instrument—the human body. We start with that.

Almost every dance school or dance technique or dance style has a recognizable vocabulary of movement, but not all of them boast terminologies that describe every step and gesture. In some cases one can describe characteristics or principles, while in others, names for key steps exist. In this last category lies tap dancing. Everyone has heard of a *time step* or a *buck-and-wing.* The student tap dancer adds to these such terms as *brush, flap, drag, shuffle, cramp roll* and the like. The viewer, to appreciate tap, need not know the name of these steps, for what he is concerned with is the ingenious way in which the dancer, or the choreographer, puts them together and the manner in which the dancer interrelates them with speed, variety and originality.

With tap it all starts with the *step*—the ball of the foot striking the floor for a single tap; two taps may follow or multiple taps. The *brush* can take the tap in any direction—forward, back, side. Add a *heel drop* and you have the sound of the heel striking the floor following one, two or more basic *step taps* by the ball of the foot. A *wing?* Shoot the foot swiftly to one side and bring it back to its starting point in the wink of an eye. A key step, the *shuffle,* is accomplished by the working foot (as distinct from the standing leg) brushing forward with a tap and back (or to the side) with a tap. Most tap terms are in themselves descriptions of the step. The tap artist pools them in many sequences and adds original movements to give a sense of improvisation to a style that should appear to be improvised unless, of course, it is done by a precision line of dancers, such as the Radio City Music Hall Rockettes.

Tap is closely associated with jazz and is most often done to jazz music. In the prejazz era, of course, it was done in ragtime or to the popular rhythms of any given era. Today it is usually jazz-related, but such great classic tapsters as Paul Draper have tap-danced to the music of Bach, and, in teaching, they intersperse ballet terminology

Tap (*Night and Days*), Laurie Ichino.

(always in French) with the lingo of tap. But although tap is a major jazz outlet in dance, it is by no means the only one. In the mid-twentieth century, something called *jazz dancing* came along, and jazz dancing has practically no terminology at all, for its roots can be in almost any established theatrical dance technique.

In Canada there is an enormously enthusiastic public for jazz ballet. This has produced a company called Les Ballets Jazz, which obviously is ballet-oriented, and a variety of jazz-dance schools in which the pupils master classical ballet as their basic discipline. In the 1940s the late Jack Cole built his jazz dances on the 2,000-year-old classical technique of the temple dances of India! And Pearl Primus, the great American specialist in the traditional dances of Africa, has performed the steps of a West African *Fanga* to the accompaniment of ancestral drums and then repeated it, without changing a step, to the tune of "As the Saints Come Marching In"! Jazz dance, then, is not a technique, it is a style, a way of dancing. It is rhythm, not step, that makes for jazz dancing.

Folk dances and ethnic art dances are the products of peoples and cultures, and not the invention of individuals, schools or academies. Ethnic art dances include both the folk element and the art expression, and they differ only in that folk dancing is the province of everyone, trained or untrained, for it is communal, recreational dance. The art dance requires the skill of the professional. In ethnic dance there is no universal terminology, since these dances are as varied as the languages and dialects spoken by their originators and continuing celebrants. Thus the terminology of the classic dances of India ranges from ancient Sanskrit—to explain the philosophies and religious concepts of the dances—to modern Hindi.

In India's *Bharata Natyam* school there are hundreds of names for the traditional vocabulary of Hindu dance gestures. And although

Song and dance—
Chita Rivera.

the dances of India are popular in America and in Europe today, there is no need for followers of Indian dance, other than students of these forms, to learn the East Indian names for the nine movements of the eyeball! It makes one feel rather superior, however, to be able to refer to that fascinating Hindu neck shift, in which the head seems to slide back and forth across the shoulders as a *sundari* and to know that the gestures themselves exist under the encompassing name of *mudras*.

Spanish dance, an ethnic form that ranges from simple village *jotas* to brilliantly choreographed *jotas* for the theater, from flamenco songs and dances performed by families to the intricate flamenco measures of great Spanish dance stars, has a fairly large list of terms. Yet they don't cover all the steps and stances. Some terms are simply Spanish translations of French ballet terms (*assamble* for *assemblé*, *cabriola* for *cabriole, pas de buret* for *pas de bourrée*), but there are strictly Spanish expressions that will describe a step or a classification of steps. *Taconeo* is a word for classification, since it is the term for foot beats, including beats with the heel, the toe and the full foot. A *desplante* is a flat stamp, a *pica* is a stamp of the ball of the foot, and a *zapateado,* which can be a sequences of steps or an entire dance, takes *taconeo* and exploits its possibilities in every possible rhythmic combination. Clap your hands? *Palmadas.* Snap your fingers? *Pito.*

Around the world, dance terminologies vary language by language to indicate steps, gestures, patterns and positions characteristic of a myriad of traditions and styles. Japan, China, Indonesia, Burma are distinctly different in their dances and dance terms, yet all are Oriental. The same applies to other continents and their cultures.

In folk dance even the untrained eye can distinguish familiar steps and patterns. A Bulgarian chain dance, whatever it is called in Sofia or Varna, is recognizable as a chain, a *stomp* is a stomp in any language, and if as an American you're an expert at dancing the Virginia Reel, be assured that you already know the steps and formations of England's Sir Roger de Coverley—something that happened in 1776 caused a change of name but not of step!

There have been attempts, off and on, to see if an acceptable terminology could be assembled for American's modern dance. Nothing satisfactory has emerged, for modern dance is not a school like ballet or *Bharata Natyam;* it is a concept of dance. The forebears, the pioneers of American's contemporary dance—Isadora

Duncan, Ruth St. Denis and, a little later, Ted Shawn—had dreams of what they thought the "new" dance would be, but they had no names for special movements. The next generation of American modern dancers was not only concerned with concepts and ideals, but with technical advancement. Each, however, had a highly individual approach to the nascent art. Martha Graham classified movements in the categories of contraction (of muscles) and release (return to natural state), while German-born Hanya Holm divided hers into tension and relaxation. Doris Humphrey, exploring the forces of gravity, was concerned with fall and recovery. But these are principles of movement, not terminologies of steps and movements.

Most modern dancers, when teaching, use French ballet terms mingled with specific instructions in English: "flex the foot," "twist the torso," "show me a succession up the spine," "step-leap-step-leap, fall backward." Martha Graham dancers and dance students know a kick as "the 'Cave' kick," but it has nothing whatever to do with a cave nor does it look like one. It was used in a dance work by Miss Graham called *Cave of the Heart* (1946), and it is referred to as "cave" simply because it started there. So the term *cave kick* means nothing either to a non-Graham student or to the public. But when you see it, it is wonderful: a sweeping high kick that describes a great arc in space; it can be joyous or angry or terrified or ecstatic, depending on how it is done and where it is done. What it is called is of no concern to us.

Ballet, the classical dance art of the Western world, is quite another matter. Its terminology is reasonably standard. There are a few minor differences of interpretation between schools or teachers, but these do not interfere with the universality of ballet training. The terminology is French and is understood in every country where ballet is taught, although teachers and pupils may not know a word of French other than those used in the ballet classroom.

To understand the terminology of ballet, to appreciate the classical style, to savor the elaborate technique of this form of dance which today has achieved a world popularity undreamed of in the past, one must know where ballet came from, how it developed over the centuries, and in what respects the ballet dancer differs from other dancers. To look at ballet with knowledgeable eyes and to get the most out of it, we must look briefly at its history.

Watching classical ballet, we see a body. This dancer's body seems leaner, more muscled than ours. However, it is completely

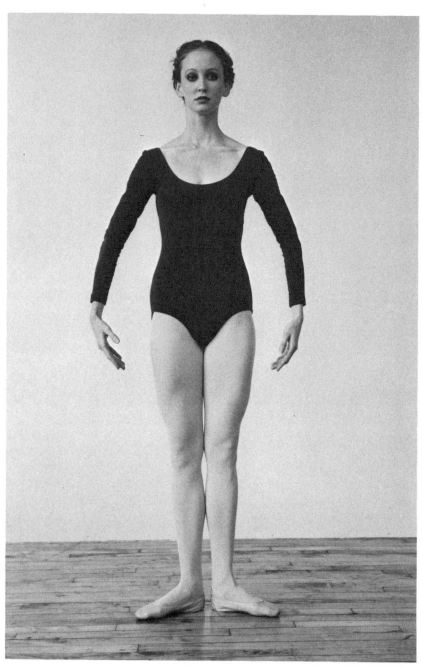

Five classic positions of the feet—Michaela Hughes (first, second, third, fourth, fifth). Fifth position shown arms high (*en haute*).

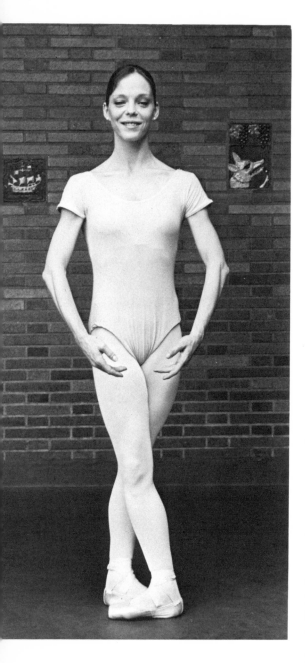

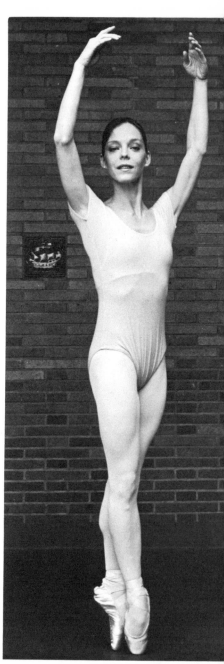

Fifth position—Rebecca
Wright—arms low (*en bas*).

Fifth position, on toe (*sur les pointes*), arms high (*en haute*).

recognizable. Then it begins to move. The lower limbs are turned out to a remarkable degree—all hips are rotary, and we have the potential to turn out to the same degree. There are walks, runs, jumps, leaps, turns, familiar actions to *every* body, but the ballet dancer executes them differently. The difference is rooted in a discipline called technique and in a manner known as style.

Classical ballet technique and style had their origins in movements that anyone could do. In Europe in the Middle Ages, peasants danced. So did courtiers—kings and princes, dukes and knights, poets and warriors. Dances are born of the people, and as they move from village square or barn or field and shore to mansions and palaces, they are refined and augmented by actions concerned with etiquette.

Ballet had its formal beginnings in fêtes, banquets and ceremonial occasions at the ducal courts of Italy. There were dance interludes, pantomimes, songs and verses extolling the virtues and exploits of the local duke or his guest. Allegorical figures from Greek mythology served to get these messages of aggrandizement across; sometimes these figures also served food, for certainly deities of the sea would dance in with the fish course, and Diana, goddess of the hunt, would be responsible for venison. Wine? Bacchus, of course!

Looking at ballet today, you will see precious little food, unless you count the candy canes and marzipan in George Balanchine's staging of *The Nutcracker,* but you will see something of the high etiquette of the royal and ducal courts as the ballerina curtseys to the floor and the *premier danseur* acknowledges her presence with that *grand révérence* once reserved for monarchs. When Catherine de Medici, Queen Mother of France, presented her *Ballet Comique de la Reine* to an audience of thousands of notables assembled in her palace in 1581, she and her guests were viewing dances they all knew and loved to perform themselves. The Italian-born Queen Mother had introduced ballet-tinged spectacle to France on a major scale—it had filtered into court entertainment earlier—but it remained for the next century's Louis XIV to make ballet professional.

In ballets produced by command of the king and danced by himself and members of his court, the steps were those used in the social dances of the day, such as the *pavane,* the *gaillard,* the *gigue,* the *passepied* and so on. These had once been peasant dances—it takes only elegance to transform a jig into a *gigue*—adopted and then adapted for courtiers. The next stage was to develop the steps in such court dances and enhance them for professional performance. Louis XIV when he danced in court ballets—his favorite role was that of Apollo, an association which led him to be referred to as "The Sun King"—most certainly pointed his toes and assumed stances with those toes turned out to allow for graceful tread. Much later, when the ballet school which Louis established produced professional dancers rather than graceful amateurs, the ballet dancer would seek to achieve a ninety-degree turnout of the legs, which was made possible by exercising the rotary properties of the hip and not by twisting and tormenting the knee.

With the balletic turnout, it was possible to move swiftly and facilely in any direction—sideways (without tripping over one's feet) as well as front and back and on diagonals. Simple walking turns became *pirouettes,* glides became *glissades,* and other steps from the court dances slowly evolved into the movement vocabulary of the classical ballet.

Taking a quick look at how rules of technique and mastery of style began, we learn that Louis established l'Académie Royale de la Danse in 1661 as a sort of exploratory commission to formulate and suggest methods of training dancers; in 1669 the king established l'Académie Royale de la Musique and had a school of dance incorporated into it in 1672; in 1681 the products of that school, headed by the world's first professional ballerina, a Mlle. Lafontaine, performed and the Paris Opéra Ballet was born.

Lafontaine probably did little more than her courtly predecessors, for she wore court dress with hoopskirts to the floor, high-heeled shoes, elaborate wigs and hats. But what she did, she did better than her amateur forebears. With professionalism, however, competition arose, and the female dancers sought to match the male dancers (far less encumbered by heavy dress) and to surpass each other.

While striving for the extension of technical facility, dancers did not lose sight of the need for expressive movement. Yes, their dances were *entrées* (separate dances related only loosely to the plot of an opera) composed of the familiar *passepieds* and *chaconnes* (early court dances), presented throughout productions where plot was principally the concern of the opera artists. But there were those dancers who strove for dramatic effect as well as for physical skill. One such was Françoise Prévost who came along shortly after Lafontaine. She reigned as *première danseuse* at the Paris Opéra for about thirty years. It was said of her that "composers write *passepieds* because Mlle. Prévost dances them with such fluent elegance." But in 1708 she and her partner, Jean Balon, became major ballet innovators when they mimed the last act of Corneille's classical play, *Les Horaces*. No words were spoken. The event was described by an observer: "They vitalized their gestures and the play of facial expression to such a degree that they caused tears to flow."

For three centuries ballet, ballet dancers and balletomanes have sought a balance between physical virtuosity and expressivity. Whenever an imbalance occurred, the art declined, and drastically. Prévost's immediate successors at the Paris Opéra came to symbolize two contrasting yet complementary approaches to ballet. Marie Camargo (1710–1770) was concerned with the steps, the technique, the prowess of the dancer. Envious of the male's ability to move athletically because of his nonrestricting costume, she shortened her skirts (to lower-calf length) so that her skillful footwork could be admired, and she took the heels off her slippers so that she could spring into the air with the ease of a man.

Her contemporary and only rival was Marie Sallé. She too modified her dress by ridding herself of hoopskirts and panniers, freeing her head of decorative impedimenta so that her hair fell loosely, and dressing almost as simply as Isadora Duncan would two centuries later. But her reasons were wholly different from those of Camargo. She was not interested in intricate steps or in rivaling the male in matters of virtuosity. She was an actress-dancer—and ballet's first female choreographer—and for her tremendously successful creation, *Pygmalion* (1734), she wanted to look like a figure from classical Greece and not from an eighteenth-century French court. And she wished to be free to move her limbs with gestural simplicity and eloquence.

Camargo and Sallé each had her own ardent following and each added to the vocabulary of classical ballet—one in terms of physical technique, the other in terms of dramatic verity. In the centuries ahead when one of these two balletic lines was neglected, the art itself faltered, as it has done cyclically on several occasions. Early in this century the need for reform was repeated when Isadora Duncan and Ruth St. Denis rebelled against the classical ballet because it was concerned with little else but steps and triviality of theme. As late as the 1930s, John Martin, the dance critic of *The New York Times,* invented names for two dance categories: He described ballet as "spectacular dance" and modern dance as "expressional dance."

There is no reason today, however, why ballet cannot incorporate within its actions the spectacular and the expressive, just as modern dance has taken on increased virtuosity garnered from a closer association with ballet technique.

Today's ballet student and even the ballet star attend class each morning or afternoon, and often both. On these occasions they are almost totally concerned with things physical. The novice, however, takes the classroom exercises on stage while the star leaves the *air* of the classroom behind as she or he creates, for the public, the *aura* of theater.

The glamour of the theater is not present in dance studios except in the persons of glamorous stars. And even here glamour is considerably dampened by sweat, for your Giselle or Princess Aurora or Prince Charming does indeed sweat. For centuries now, the hands of generations of those who dance such glittering roles have rested lightly every day on a ballet *barre* in Paris, St. Petersburg or Philadelphia. The limbs have been turned out to that (at first) uncomfortable ninety-degree position and the body pulled erect so that there is an unseen but real plumb line established from the crown of the head to the union of the two heels, a union achieved as the exact back of each heel presses against the other in ballet's first position. There are five positions of the feet, and throughout the entire class, whether it lasts for an hour, an hour and a half (the standard length) or longer, every exercise, every movement, will begin from one of these positions and terminate in one of them. Whether the ballerina or beginning student bends, glides, steps, turns, jumps, leaps, or beats or executes combinations thereof, the five positions are inescapable.

Why should the viewer care about the five positions? Keeping track of them while the performer is moving through the choreo-

Drama and mood coupled with fourth position *sur les pointes*—Gelsey Kirkland rehearses *The Dying Swan.*

36

graphic intricacies of a variation from *Swan Lake* or *The Nutcracker* could be turned into a game—yes, he did a double turn in air and landed in a perfect fifth or . . . no, he missed it! But to know the details of ballet technique is not necessary for the viewer. Listening to an opera aria, one does not need to know the intervals in the song—the layman can hear a note that is flat or sharp or on pitch. The same is true with ballet—a sloppy finish to a *pirouette,* a stagger after an air turn, a fumble after a balancing on *pointe* are clearly discernible as wrong. When a movement is done correctly, it will sell itself.

What is achieved theatrically, aesthetically or purposefully through technical accomplishment is important. One of the most famous (and difficult) dances in all classical ballet is "The Rose Adagio" in *The Sleeping Beauty.* The sixteen-year-old Princess Aurora is courted by four cavaliers. Her parents, a king and queen, watch as she dances with these princes, for perhaps she will select one as a suitable husband. For two extended periods within the framework of this adagio, the ballerina balances on a single *pointe* while the other leg is raised to the side and back in a position known as *attitude.* One arm is raised above the head; the other is held by a cavalier who supports her as she stands. Then, in turn, each cavalier steps forward to press his suit, and as she changes hands from one prince to another, she lets go of her support for a second as she raises the previously supported hand over her head to match her already raised arm in a lovely oval curve that frames her head (this would be a "high" fifth position for the arms).

At the very close of the adagio—earlier each cavalier has presented her with a single rose as she danced, and now they do so once again—she steps lightly onto *pointe* and into an immediate *attitude.* But this time she not only balances alone between each proferred hand, but she is turned once around in a promenade by each cavalier before she relinquishes his hand and repeats her solo balance in the high fifth position prior to accepting the hand of her next cavalier. These moments can be breathtaking, scary, boring or disastrous.

The act of balancing unattended is itself a challenge to the dancer and generally eyecatching for the average viewer. But there is much, much more to it—for doer as well as viewer—than proving a control of that plumb line through the center of the body. As used in "The Rose Adagio," these two sequences cannot be done like, or regarded as, a trick. There must be no sign of tension or insecurity, for this is no longer a female dancer practicing balances at the impersonal ballet *barre*. Here is a PRINCESS. For her nothing is difficult, nothing impossible. She is engaged in what she is doing because she wants to do so, because it amuses her to do so, because it is taking place at *her* pleasure—and if it is so performed, it will be done to *your* pleasure also.

Perhaps the greatest Princess Aurora of this century was Margot Fonteyn. The illusion she created was unforgettable. Even at fifty years old, she seemed to be no more than sixteen, for in her smile was the radiance of youth. Technically the balances caused her no trouble at all, so the first hurdle was passed easily. Next, she didn't want the Rose Adagio's balances to look like nothing more than a physical feat. Of course, the challenge was present, but Fonteyn made the viewer believe that a fairy-tale princess was above the law, including the law of gravity. In those instants of balance, she had placed herself upon a pedestal where her suitors could see her clearly. It simply happened that the pedestal was made not of marble but of her own satin-shod, delicate foot. The two fatally bad extremes of execution were absent from these balances; she neither pawed the air frantically between "catches" nor did she show off with a sort of "Look, Ma, no hands!" performance. The point of the *pointe* here is to achieve a portrait, etched in dance, of a beautiful young girl poised on the threshold of her first romance.

The huge vocabulary of classical ballet, controlled but never constricted by rules of technique, can speak soundlessly yet clearly to us all whether we are assembled in a theater or movie house or comfortably settled in front of a television screen. It may communicate to us through a number of styles: romantic, dramatic, comic, fantastic, realistic, surrealistic, semiabstract, abstract. Yes, even abstract, nonstory dances can have meanings that have nothing whatever to do with either characterization or narrative. And yes, steps and movements taken right from the classroom can be molded into new, unexpected and exciting choreographic forms.

For more than half a century, George Balanchine has delighted, startled and stirred vast audiences in the theater and on the TV screen with ballet movements that you could find defined and diagrammed in any book on classical ballet. But he puts them together in sequences we have never before seen; inspired always by music, he touches them with colors and invests them with dynamic

Abstract design in choreography—Balanchine's *Serenade*
with Dance Theatre of Harlem.

intensities born of his musical stimuli; he arranges them in different
speeds, accords them moments of rest; with an ensemble he can use
these movements in patterns that are uniform or asymmetrical, he
can direct them into canon forms as simple and charming as "Three
Blind Mice" or weave them into contrapuntal patterns that Bach
would have cheered.

A dictionary of words is there for a writer's or speaker's reference,
and rules of grammar provide him with helpful, not hindering,
disciplines. The technique behind the world's great literature is there
in the dictionary, the grammar, the thesaurus. The technique behind
the world's great ballet choreography is in the vocabulary used daily
in the classroom. How it is used, how it is viewed: therein lies the
magic of ballet.

Can you imagine yourself being transported into a world of magic
by the most common infinitive found in English grammar? Of course

not. And yet . . . have you ever listened to John Barrymore, John Gielgud, Richard Burton or Laurence Olivier saying, "TO BE OR NOT TO BE." If Shakespeare worked this grammatical miracle for his Hamlet, it is not beyond comprehension that a master choreographer, Michel Fokine, could take one of ballet's oldest and most familiar steps, the *pas de bourrée,* and transform it into the pulsating heart of the most famous ballet solo the world has ever known, *Le Cygne,* known to everyone as the immortal Pavlova's *The Dying Swan.*

3 How to Look at

Supported *arabesque*—the Dayton Ballet Company's *The Sleeping Beauty* with Christine O'Neal and Richard Stutzman.

Ballet

Anna Pavlova, in 1905, needed a short, modest solo for a charity event at which she had promised to perform. She went to a young choreographer with rebellious ideas about a "new" approach to ballet, Michel Fokine (1880–1942), and asked him to make a dance for her. It took only "a few minutes," as Fokine later recalled, for him to create *The Dying Swan*. She walked behind him in the studio as he indicated movements of the feet, the arms, the body. Nothing spectacular was required of the feet. The key step, the *pas de bourrée*, is nothing more than a series of tiny steps swiftly done. And done perfectly, as Pavlova did them, they could be described as a strand of pearls falling in shimmering sequence on a polished table or floor. But the body was alive with shimmering motion too. Here was an early clue to the "new" Fokine approach to ballet which was to replace exploitation of mere technique with dancing that would touch the soul and the emotions of the spectator and not simply the eye.

It was this brief solo, as danced by Pavlova, that symbolized the reawakening of America's interest in ballet, for until the first of the Russian ballerina's performances in America in 1910, ballet had slumbered for more than half a century. *The Dying Swan,* presented in tours both in concert and vaudeville over the years, stirred the public and aroused legions of mothers to enroll their daughters in ballet classes.

Little girls and adults have attempted to dance *The Dying Swan* for decades. Not even their ineptitude can destroy it, and it remains, in the care of great dancers, a masterwork of choreography. The continuous *bourrées,* danced smoothly, glidingly, then tremulously and finally brokenly, represent the flow of life, the shadow of death and death itself. The onlooker may not be consciously aware of identifying himself with a doomed bird, but that is what is happening as we watch in fascination a life ebbing away.

Fokine's choreography is masterful in its very simplicity. The streaming *bourrées* are interrupted briefly by pauses, balances that mirror the alertness of a living creature sensitive to the presence of danger. Then, at the end, there is a desperate reach for life, a fall into defeat, the acceptance of death.

There are many interpretations of *The Dying Swan*. Pavlova's is

The Dying Swan—
Maya Plisetskaya (Bolshoi Ballet).

Arabesque—Makarova
as Odette in *Swan Lake*
(American Ballet Theatre).

preserved through old movies made in the 1920s. Alicia Markova (born Lilian Alicia Marks in London in 1910) as a child dancer was dubbed "the miniature Pavlova," so much did she resemble a doll-like version of the great Russian ballerina. Markova, destined to become England's first great ballerina, later modeled her own world-famous performance of *The Dying Swan* after Pavlova's own. Still later, Nathalie Krassovska, half-Scottish, half-Russian, learned *The Dying Swan* from Fokine himself in the late 1930s when she was a star of the Ballet Russe de Monte Carlo. Her version, therefore, would be a definitive one. But other dancers have used the Pavlova-

Fokine original as a base for more personal adaptations. Among these are the Bolshoi Ballet's dazzling Maya Plisetskaya, who offers a version that is highly individual—her undulating arms remind one of the arm ripples Ruth St. Denis used in her Oriental dances—and with it, she has hypnotized audiences around the world with her remarkable portrait of inevitable mortality.

Most choreographers and dancers use the word *movement* to indicate a step or some sort of body action. George Balanchine instead elects to use the word *gesture* to mean movement. Since Balanchine's creations are frequently abstract, without story or plot,

Arabesques
(clockwise from
lower left):
accent down . . .
accent out . . .
accent up . . .
penché . . .
dramatic.

gesture would seem to be an odd synonym for the kind of movement he employs. For although the dictionary defines the word as "a movement of the body, head, arms, hands or face," it incorporates into that definition the requirement that a gesture be "expressive of an idea, opinion, emotion." The gestures, mainly pantomimic, that Giselle uses in her Mad Scene—tossing her loosened hair wildly, pretending to pick petals off nonexistent daisies, running frantically as if to escape from the knowledge that she has been betrayed—express emotion. When she rips off the necklace given her by the princess as she learns that the former is also betrothed to her perfidious lover, she expresses an opinion. Balanchine rarely expresses opinion through his movements and only occasionally does he use gesture-movement to indicate emotion. When he does, it is an exhilarating experience. But all his movements (that is, gestures) are expressive of the concept of "idea."

George Balanchine, born and schooled in Russia, left his homeland (as Fokine had done nearly twenty years earlier) in 1924. With fresh choreographic ideas he joined Serge Diaghilev's Ballets Russes (1909–1929) in Paris as the last of that impresario's great choreographers (that is, Fokine, Nijinsky, Massine, Nijinska, Balanchine) whose individual gifts he promoted. In 1933 Balanchine came to America. It was here, first as head of the School of American Ballet and as chief choreographer of several companies (culminating in today's New York City Ballet), that he developed his concept of non-narrative ballets.

But whether a ballet tells a story or hints at moods, or is an abstract, geometric, patterned extension of music into shapes, its classical steps are open to a variety of uses and interpretations.

An *arabesque,* one of the most common yet most beautiful movements in ballet, always expresses (or should) an idea. So it is not enough for the dancer to say, "Oh, I do an *arabesque* here," or for someone looking at dance to say, "Oh, that's an *arabesque*." For an *arabesque* can express an endless array of ideas. What *kind* of *arabesque* is it? Is it tilted down, out or up? Is the back leg placed high or low? Is the standing leg on *pointe, demi-pointe* or flat? Where are the arms held? How is the head held? The position itself, even in its most classical guise, has many possibilities. Where does the *arabesque* come in a "sentence of movement"? Who is doing the *arabesque*? Is the dancer alone? What is the costume worn by the dancer? What is the period of the ballet?

Supported *arabesque*—Balanchine's *Stars and Stripes*—Merrill Ashley, Peter Martins (New York City Ballet).

That step, that position, that movement, that gesture we term *arabesque* can have as many meanings as the word *love*: "I love you" or "I *love* you" or "I love *you*"; "I love you" as addressed to your mate, your child, your grandmother; "I love chocolate"; "Love Me or Leave Me"; "I could not love thee, dear, so much, loved I not honour more"; "Oh, my luve is like a red, red rose"; or "Liebestod" (Love death). The potential uses for the word *love* and for the movement *arabesque* are endless.

The dancer, in executing an *arabesque,* stands on one leg with the other leg extended back in a straight line (the knee is not bent). The classic turnout in the hips is of course retained, and the arms may be placed in any one of several classical *port-de-bras* positions.

First, an *arabesque* is a design in space. If the body presenting it is attractive and the *arabesque* is done correctly, it has aesthetic value simply as design. But what of the space in which it exists? As Jerome Robbins has said, "Space is not emptiness; it is volume." Try to run against the wind, and you'll realize he is right—you cannot see air but it is there in space. Gravity is also present, although you cannot see it. Gravity is what makes it possible for you to fall; in middle age it accounts for slowly sagging buttocks. The *arabesque,* because it is

Supported *penché
arabesque*—
Makarova and
son, André.

fashioned with a balance on one leg, tempts the pull of gravity while it carves its pattern out of the invisible volume that is space.

By tilting the body slightly forward and directing the glance downward, the dancer in *arabesque* can make the viewer aware of the space surrounding the lower part of the body. This stance may suggest the pull of gravity or, in a planned sequence of movement, sadness, depression or isolation of self. With the head erect and facing forward and with an arm, or both arms, reaching forth, the *arabesque* becomes outgoing, the pull of gravity remains unaccented and a thrust forward suggests that the *arabesque* is not simply a design in space but a movement going somewhere. With the head lifted upward, the chest raised accordingly, an arm stretch directed skyward, the *arabesque* points to the space above the body, to the heavens, to the stars, to flight, to freedom from the fetters of gravity, to release (or the desire for release).

Arabesque images in ballet are plentiful: the exuberant Swanilda in *Coppélia* reaching out for fun and mischief; Giselle (in Act I) poised joyously on the threshold of romance and (in Act II) in a deep *arabesque* directed toward the earth from which she has emerged as a ghost and to which she must return; Odette, Queen of the Swans, in an *arabesque* that is a pause in flight; the playful *arabesque* of the Sylphide as James tries to capture her; Lizzie Borden, in *Fall River Legend,* stabbing the floor with an angry *arabesque* as her hands beat the empty air in frustration. Or is the *arabesque* that moment when the Prince, in his soliloquy in *Swan Lake,* steps forth as he reaches out and up in a desperate search for his destiny?

It is possible to take any movement found in the vocabulary of classical ballet and illustrate its manifold uses, its multiple meanings. The *arabesque,* or its first cousin, the *attitude,* can be the starting step or the culminating step in a movement phrase, or it can, in the middle of a danced sentence, be a passing step that in a *pas de deux* leads the ballerina right into her cavalier's arms or, conversely, serves as a mode of escape from unwanted embraces.

In ballet, as indeed in any form of theater dance, there are two poles that must be established by the dancer and recognized by the audience. At one end is simply standing (or it could be sitting or lying down), and at the other end is a movement burst of some sort, such as an explosive jump, a soaring leap, a dizzying spin. But for the theater, standing must become a stance. The audience should be able to tell at first glance if the dancer is playing a peasant girl, a princess, a queen, an innocent, a vamp, or a slut. When the Prince in *Swan Lake* sits on a throne to observe six maidens who are potential brides, he is trying to decide which one, if any, would be acceptable as a wife. When Apollo, in Balanchine's ballet *Apollo* (1928), sits in a sacred grove and observes three Muses dancing for him, he is not judging a beauty contest, he is in the awesome service of the gods themselves.

Mother Simone in Jean Dauberval's *La Fille Mal Gardée* (1789) has her hands firmly planted on her hips, arms akimbo: Don't tangle with her. The dance-hall girls in Eugene Loring's *Billy the Kid* (1938) have their hands on their hips but resting there lightly and pressing down toward their buttocks: Feel free to tangle with them. Hagar in Antony Tudor's *Pillar of Fire* (1942) sits on the steps of her Victorian home with her virginal knees pressed tightly together, back primly erect. Zobeide, in Fokine's *Schéhérazade* (1910), sprawls on her harem pillow, her back invitingly arched. Billy the Kid himself stands erect, defiant of the world, unafraid. The Golden Slave in *Schéhérazade* stands in a crouch at his entrance from his cell, hopeful in the lift of his head, still fearful in the unobtrusive slink of his body.

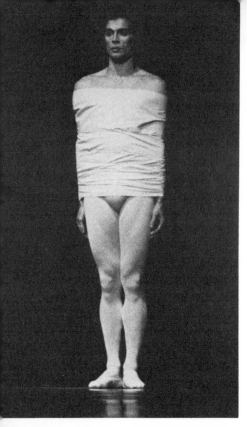

Moments from Balanchine's *Apollo*
with Nureyev: the child god . . .
the young god (with Pippa Wilde and
Wendy Groombridge as two muses)
. . . with the muse Terpsichore (Merle Park)
. . . with the three muses
. . . hearing the call of the gods—
Apollo with the three muses.
(Various casts and companies shown.)

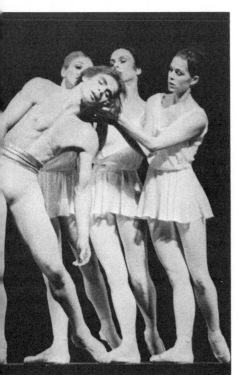

Clog dance by Mother Simone (Jacques Gorrissen) in Ashton's *La Fille Mal Gardée* (National Ballet of Canada).

Madge, the witch, in an old ballet of the Romantic Age, August Bournonville's Danish version of *La Sylphide* (1836), is introduced to us as a stooped, shuffling figure. We hardly notice her entrance into the festivities at the Scottish engagement party. As she sits, huddled over the palms she is reading, she seems mysterious, perhaps even ominous, but when in anger she stands erect with arms outflung to deliver a curse, she is terrifying. The stance is the clue to a characterization, the key, very often, to the action to follow.

When Pamela May was the principal mime of Britain's Royal Ballet, she numbered among her acting roles the Princess-Mother in the Petipa-Ivanov *Swan Lake* (1895), the Queen in Petipa's *The Sleeping Beauty* (1890) and a Princess in Jean Coralli's *Giselle* (1841). In all three ballets she did little more than walk, except for some pantomime passages, and large sections of the walks required that she be accompanied by a male. The novice dancer would say, "I'm royal and I walk," and settle for that. Not Miss May. As she pointed out to me in an interview some years ago, each was different from the other. "In *Swan Lake*, I'm the sovereign, the ruler. In *The Sleeping Beauty*, I'm the consort of the ruler who is the King. In *Giselle*, I'm the daughter of a prince." Pamela May made the distinctions clear in her performances. Her tread as the Princess-Mother was authoritative, and when she placed her hand on her son's arm, it was a command for him to escort her. In *Beauty* she moved regally but unobtrusively alongside the King, and her hand was placed on his arm with dutiful affection. In the hunting party in *Giselle*, she was simply led through the forest to the clearing by her protective father. The stance, the step, the placement of a hand are essential to the correct doing and the rewarding viewing of a role.

Probably the most quoted line from the writings of Gertrude Stein is "A rose is a rose is a rose." The student-dancer is likely to say, "A

Sitting—rehearsing Tudor's *Pillar of Fire*
(Rebecca Wright)—at rest, ready.

An exotic sit—*Schéhérazade*—
Virginia Johnson as the harem favorite,
Zobeide (Dance Theatre of Harlem).

turn is a turn is a turn." Not so. A turn can be done in a single spot, it can be a traveling turn, it can be done high in the air, it can be both aerial and travel out as well as up. It can be the climax of a phrase of movement or simply a preparation for something that is to follow.

In Balanchine's abstract *Symphony in C,* there is a place where the ballerina does three consecutive *pirouettes* at allegro speed. She executes the first and snaps it into an end pose that is partly diagonal; she repeats this but with a shift in direction along another diagonal; last, she ends on the third *pirouette,* full front. These are extensions of the bright notes of Bizet's music into movement. You "see" the sounds; they are sharp, bright, brilliant. It is abundantly clear why this ballet's initial title was *Le Palais de Cristal,* for the movement in these turns is crystalline.

In a ballet such as *La Sylphide* or in the later *Les Sylphides* (1907) (inspired by the former), both evocations of Romantic Ballet, the turns are softer, unhurried, as if the dancers were stirred by gentle breezes or as if a dancer would linger on the very lilt of a turn. In contrast, there is a scene in Valerie Bettis's version of Tennessee Williams's *A Streetcar Named Desire* (1952) when the heroine throws herself into violent turns as she thrusts her arms out in self-protection. Once, when this ballet was danced by Nora Kaye and Igor Youskevitch, the latter stepped too close and was knocked out cold on stage. These *Streetcar pirouettes* were obviously not those of the shepherdess in *The Nutcracker* (1892). The basic steps were the same, but the usage totally different.

Within the framework of classical ballet, there are different types of dancing. There are the mimes who stand (in character), walk (in proper period style) and employ ballet's traditional pantomimic gestures to say, for example, "I am giving a ball at the castle, there will be several beautiful girls and there will be dancing, you are to

select one of these for your bride and that's an order!" (the Princess-Mother to her son, Prince Siegfried, in *Swan Lake*). There are the character dancers who perform the national dances—*mazurkas, czardas,* Spanish-flavored dances—in the old classics. And there are the *demi-caractère* dancers (who often have the best of the ballet bargain) who combine folk or comedic qualities with fairly elaborate classical ballet technique. Albrecht in *Giselle* is considered a classical role, while Franz in Arthur Saint-Léon's *Coppélia* (1870) is *demi-caractère* mainly because the latter engages in buffoonery, kicks up his heels playfully and feels free to dance a *czardas.* In matters of balletic virtuosity, Franz has a more demanding role than Albrecht, but he doesn't have to be elegant, serious, elitist or "pure" in matters of execution.

The delightful ribbon dance for Lise and Colin in *La Fille Mal Gardée,* be it the old Russian version or Sir Frederick Ashton's contemporary staging, is classical in step but gaily *demi-caractère* in spirit as the two young peasants make a game of lovemaking. In Act IV of Marius Petipa's *La Bayadère* (1877) there is a duet passage with a filmy scarf for the ballerina and the *danseur,* but the steps are pure *ballet d'école* (that is, classically correct steps as taught in ballet

Crouch—*Schéhérazade*—Eddie Shellman
as the Golden Slave.

The curse—*La Sylphide*—Erik Bruhn as Madge, the witch, and Nureyev as James (National Ballet of Canada).

Pantomime—"I vow"—*Swan Lake*, Act Three; Nureyev as the Prince, Gregory as Odile (the black swan), Lucia Chase as the Prince's mother, Marcos Paredes as the evil magician (American Ballet Theatre).

Reach—Nureyev as the Prince in *Swan Lake*.

class), the scarf is a romantically conceived extension of that mist connecting reality with dreams.

The scarf used in the final duet of La Sylphide is poisoned. In the eyes of James it was intended to unite him with his elusive love, the Sylphide, but it was prepared by Madge, the witch, to separate the two forever. The ribbon in Fille is employed to suggest the fun of romance; the filmy scarf in Bayadère, the poetry of romance; the fatal scarf in Sylphide, the tragedy of romance. Here is a prop that serves, very differently, the demi-caractère ballet, the classical ballet, the romantic-dramatic ballet. The red-ribbon dance in the Soviet The Red Poppy (1927), if you care to pursue the potential of the ribbon-scarf in ballet, may be said to hail the joys of communism.

Obviously these ribbon and scarf dances are performed differently, not simply because the choreography varies, but because the characters involved are of various social strata and behavioral types, and because the styles of the ballets concerned are as different as, say, such operas as The Bartered Bride, Orfeo ed Euridice, La Bohème and Mahagonny. They are performed differently and viewed differently.

These styles in ballet are important variations on the art itself. The schools established in Paris and ultimately in other world capitals in the late seventeenth century and throughout the eighteenth century can be considered as headquarters for classical ballet—as they remain to this day—and what was transported from those classrooms to the stage in that first period is also classical, partly because it was first and partly because the themes of the ballets themselves were almost always drawn from classical sources. The ballets were peopled with gods and goddesses, heroes and heroines of Greek and Roman mythology.

Ballet, like painting, falls into historical and stylistic periods. From today's vantage point we can see that they consist of the first (and almost forgotten) "classic" period (1680–1800); the Romantic Age of Ballet (1800–1860); the second classic ballet era established in Imperial Russia (1860–1910); contemporary ballet (1910–the present). The first change occurred, of course, when the gods and heroes gave way to people.

As the French Revolution approached, the ordinary man and woman began to be celebrated in ballet—La Fille Mal Gardée from 1789 is the prime example of this change—and with the introduction

Demi-caractère—Coppélia (with Nureyev).

of dancing *sur les pointes* for women at the start of the nineteenth century, choreographers turned from the myths of antiquity to European legends rooted in folklore. Thus with Filippo Taglioni's *La Sylphide,* danced by his daughter Marie Taglioni, the so-called Romantic Age of Ballet was ushered in. The year was 1832. (Bournonville's Danish staging of *La Sylphide,* which survives to this day, was introduced in Copenhagen in 1836.)

A rush of Romantic Age ballets ensued; *Giselle,* destined to become the lasting symbol of the era, and all sorts of romantic excursions such as *Ondine, La Gypsy, Alma, La Fille du Danube, La Laitière Suisse, Le Diable Boiteux* and so on with sylphs, wilis, nixes, pixies and other fantastic fauna. The personal styles of four great ballerinas—Marie Taglioni, Carlotta Grisi, Fanny Cerrito, Lucile Grahn—were brought together (not without some temperamental fireworks) in a ballet entitled *Pas de Quatre,* choreographed by Jules Perrot (Grisi's dancer husband) for Queen Victoria. Sir Anton Dolin, the British *premier danseur,* has re-created this famous dance for contemporary audiences. (Dances such as *La Cracovienne,* identified with Fanny Elssler, Taglioni's major rival, have also been reconstructed for performance today.)

Demi-caractère—a ribbon dance-game, *La Fille Mal Gardée* with David Wall, Ann Jenner (Royal Ballet).

Demi-caractère—*Jockey Dans* (choreography by August Bournonville), Frank Andersen (Royal Danish Ballet).

(Below) *Pas de Quatre*—re-created by Anton Dolin with Alicia Alonso as Taglioni (standing), Maria Elena Llorente (as Grahn), Mirta Plá (as Cerrito), Marta Garcia (as Grisi) (Ballet Nacional de Cuba).

Dance-drama—*Giselle*, Act Two—with Baryshnikov
and Kirkland (American Ballet Theatre).

How did Dolin know how the Romantic Age stars danced? There
were no movies, no videotapes to record them. Notation, a dance
script, did exist and was developed by Cerrito's husband, the
dancer-choreographer Arthur Saint-Léon. This gives steps and ensemble formations for some of the dances of the period. The fanciful
lithographs of the era provide illustrations in dress and deportment
and even a suggestion of the qualities of movement. Descriptions by
critics of the period and by those who kept diaries help to fill in the
gaps.

This Romantic Age of Ballet coincided with the popularity of the
romantic novel, as represented in the works of Victor Hugo, and the
Victorian concept of woman as pure but desirable, a creature to be
cherished, protected and (as she poised on her pedestal of *pointes*)
honored as well as adored. We also know about the Romantic Age
of Ballet because it was preserved, although highly personalized, by
the ballets of Bournonville in the Kingdom of Denmark. By the
1850s the Romantic Age of Ballet was drawing to a swift end (except
in Denmark). Marius Petipa went to Russia and took some of these
ballets with him, which he rechoreographed along with creating an
incredible array of ballets that were to constitute a new age of ballet.

67

The Petipa era, from the middle of the last century to the opening years of the twentieth, is now (perhaps confusingly) referred to as "classic." His *The Sleeping Beauty, Swan Lake* (Acts I and III, with his assistant, Lev Ivanov, doing Acts II and IV), *Don Quixote,* and *La Bayadère* represent the classics for our time, since the "old" classics with their *chaconnes* and *passepieds* for Jason, Medea, Terpsichore and their associates are lost to all but ballet historians and occasional scholarly "reconstructionists."

Today's dancers, and those of us who look at them from our comfortable seats in the theater or in our own TV viewing rooms, must recognize these differences in style if they and we are to savor all the flavors available in classical-romantic ballet and its component parts of character, *demi-caractère* and pure *ballet d'école.*

In the majority of ballets by Balanchine, one should anticipate and relish movement without plot or characterization, see music as bodies become the instruments of rhythm, phrasing, melody, timbre, concord, discord, volume, shape. With August Bournonville (1805–1879) one should be prepared for passages of remarkably adept acting—Bournonville used actors from the Royal Danish Theater in his ballets and two of his ballerinas became great actresses—and don't expect lots of dizzying turns. It is said that Bournonville, as a dancer, was not fond of turns, but he jumped very well and his *batterie* (leg beats) was brilliant. Thus in Bournonville ballets you will never find the equivalent of the thirty-two lashing, cutting *fouettés* of *Swan Lake* renown, and you will rarely come across more than a double *pirouette* (even as performed by present-day male dancers, who can do six or ten or more). But you will find that the female dancer leaps more often and, hopefully, higher than in any other choreography, and that the intricate beats, including the almost impossible "dark step," should please and thrill the onlooker as much as sixty-four *fouettés!*

With the coming of new creative forces in this century, audiences (starting with the Diaghilev period) were invited to share in the new realism of Michel Fokine, or in the avant-garde experiments of Vaslav Nijinsky. They were expected to savor collaborations in one-act ballets (many of the Russian classics were five acts in length) requiring attention paid not simply to movement but to new sounds (Stravinsky and Satie's among them), new visuals in art and decoration (Picasso, Roualt, Matisse and the like) and stories or themes that had nothing to do with Greek gods or peasants or pixies

Adagio—*pas de poisson*—rehearsal with
Makarova and Alexander Godunov (*Don Quixote*).

or sleeping beauties. Totally new styles of dancing, but all performed by dancers trained in the *ballet d'école,* offered new challenges to the performer and certainly equal challenges to the aesthetic tastes of audiences.

After Serge Diaghilev and the Ballets Russes (1909–1929) came a fluctuating, expanding, experimenting period in ballet when American modern dance, vital and surging, and, to a lesser degree, European modern dance began to seep into the classical ballet arena, to inspire choreographers and to provide them with new tools with which to express their ideas. Classical ballet was supported by a

Cabriole—Baryshnikov in
Eliot Feld's *Variations on America*.

tremendous vocabulary of movement; modern dance boasted that it had *no* set vocabulairy but that it was a *concept* of movement.

What the unlikely coming together of traditional ballet and modern dance produced has made ballet history for our time. Early in this century, Pavlova, dancing Fokine's brief *The Dying Swan,* gave ballet its impetus to rebirth and changed the course of dance history. In mid-century a young, comparatively unknown American dancer, clad in an unadorned dark green dress, her hair severely combed, her mien that of a spinster, stood on the great stage of the old Metropolitan Opera House in New York City and received twenty-seven curtain calls. A star was born that night in the grand tradition of the theater, but a new style of ballet found a special apogee that same night.

The sixteen-year-old, protected, innocent Princess Aurora had been replaced, or pushed aside, by a woman who felt passion and frustration, who explored the sensually sordid while in search of a satisfying love. This was a new kind of heroine. My God, an adult! The role put new demands on the ballerina and, at the same time, reminded the audience that ballet could not only divert the viewer but stimulate and, very possibly, disturb. The ballet, of course, was Antony Tudor's *Pillar of Fire,* and the ballerina, Nora Kaye.

A great many people didn't like *Pillar of Fire* and other adult ballets—they wanted their *Sleeping Beauty* and their Tchaikovsky with feathers—but *Pillar* and other ballets by Tudor, by Agnes de Mille, by Ruth Page, the young and promising Jerome Robbins and their colleagues extended the art of ballet to new and exciting dimensions. Ballet in America had finally caught up with the motto, first depicted in massive letters above the proscenium of Copenhagen's old Royal Theater two and a half centuries ago and reproduced in later buildings serving the Royal Theater, its monarchs and its citizens: EI BLOT TIL LYST. It is there for all who enter the theater to see. It is not a warning, it is a rich, rich promise: NOT FOR PLEASURE ONLY.

4 How to Look at

Ruth St. Denis and Ted Shawn
in *Egyptian Ballet*.

Modern Dance

America's dance pioneers, at the turn of this century, knew nothing of the Royal Danish Theater's motto of NOT FOR PLEASURE ONLY, but it was just such an aesthetic that served them as a new dance creed. Paradoxically this "new" dance was to reestablish the purposes of a very "old" dance. Isadora Duncan turned to classical Greece for inspiration not to reproduce actual dances nor to use, as eighteenth-century ballet did, myths and legends for thematic material, but rather to reestablish the dance as the noblest form of human expression. With such a Hellenic heritage, there would be dances for children, youth, adults and the old; poets as well as athletes would be dancers; philosophers as well as warriors would dance.

Ruth St. Denis turned to the Orient not because she had any interest in Little Egypt and the belly dances of fairgrounds or in the *hootchy-kootchy* dancers on carnival midways, but because she had read that in ancient Egypt and in the Orient of the present there were gods who danced and people who dance about religion and the gods.

Thus Duncan and St. Denis, in rebelling against the "moribund ballet of the day" (as St. Denis described it), with its sleeping or waking princesses, pixies and butterflies, sought to reextend the ancient range of dance, restoring its potential scope from the trivial to the profound, from the secular to the sacred or the spiritual.

The very theme of Ruth St. Denis's first major creation, *Radha*, presented in New York in 1906, was a plea to dispense with pleasure. In a sense this was an exotic, dramatized sermon in dance, for in *Radha* the goddess, a bronzed figure brought to life by the faith of her followers, exhorts them in dance to renounce a life governed by the senses. Five dances explore the senses of sight, smell, hearing, taste and touch, culminating in a dance of wild abandon, "The Delirium of the Senses." But with this dance of carnal ecstasy, the figure of Radha sheds the trappings of the sensual life and returns to her dais, once more a figure of bronze, once more a symbol of a life devoted to purity, meditation, all things spiritual.

Radha had a *succès de scandale,* for press and public were either shocked or entranced or both by an Oriental costume that allowed for bare feet and legs and even for a bare midriff. Headlines in the

Isadora Duncan dances "La Marseillaise."

Boston Herald shouted "DARKNESS HID BLUSHES AS RUTH ST. DENIS DANCED." Press and public had thrilled to the trappings of Radha, but overlooked her message. Press and public, for years to come, would see the glamorous shell of the St. Denis dance-theater but rarely its contents. The audiences of 1906, and those of later years, did not know how to look at this new dance. "Barefoot maiden gives society folk a new thrill," read one report, or "Of course she's not all dressed, but it's all right to those who are Oriental."

A few had a glimmer of what St. Denis was striving for. A reporter, sounding as if he were almost surprised at himself, closed his listing

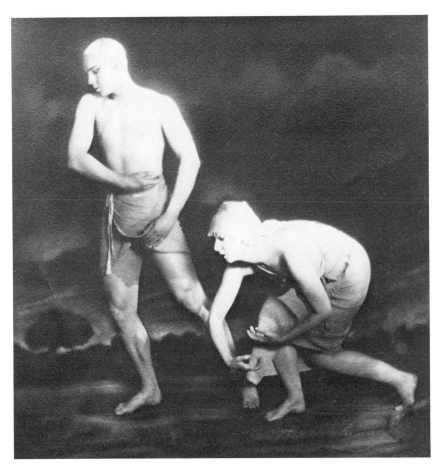

Ruth St. Denis, Ted Shawn in
"Tillers of the Soil" from *Egyptian Ballet.*

Ruth St. Denis (photographed 1906) in the
dance of "The Sense of Touch" in *Radha*.

of her physical charms with "there is something surprisingly spiritual
about her." This was echoed across the land in response to her
concert and vaudeville appearances. By 1922, eight years after she
had married Ted Shawn, made him her partner and built the
Denishawn companies and schools, press and public knew a little
bit better what to look for. They were still captured by exotic themes,
elaborate stagings and the continuing physical beauty of St. Denis
herself (although she was past forty by then), but they were
beginning to see more. A Chicago newspaper stated through its
critic, "I consider the message of the Denishawners more direct than
music, for it raises the human body to express the spiritual . . ." In
Baltimore a reporter, speaking of the duet, "Tillers of the Soil" and
"Dance of Rebirth" from the *Egyptian Ballet,* wrote: "Here was
something spiritual but real, something to cling to and remember."
And speaking of the Denishawn program as a whole, "Last night
they danced as we have never seen them dance before; danced with
body, soul and brain."

There were, of course, movement principles that differed drastically from the rules of classical ballet. To begin with, neither
Duncan nor St. Denis employed a set vocabulary of movement or

St. Denis in the Babylonian ballet,
Ishtar of the Seven Gates.

pursued academic training programs. For them each dance invited new movements which would express the ideas of that specific dance. New movements, new patterns were created under the stimulus of a musical note, phrase or composition, or under the stimulus of a dramatic incident, theme, story, site, period in time or—simply—a kinetic idea.

It seemed to both St. Denis and Duncan that classical ballet focused upon the limbs rather than upon the trunk of the body. Since that trunk was the central body part, the biggest unit, and since it housed the body's vital organs, the two young rebels sought for a

Ted Shawn and his Men Dancers
in *Kinetic Molpai*.

center of movement impulse in that area. Duncan, in a fanciful but fascinating image, suggested that "the soul" resided in "the solar plexus." In more acceptable kinesiological terms, she decided that this central area of the body was "the crater of motor power."

St. Denis, likewise concerned with the articulation of the central part of the body, began also to explore breath rhythms. Degrees of depth in inhalation, phrasing through breath were factors she considered important to the drama of dance, to the conveying of emotional states of being.

Both Duncan and St. Denis had been exposed in childhood to

Barton Mumaw of the Shawn Dancers in the "Dance of the Banner Bearer" in *Olympiad*.

Doris Humphrey with the Humphrey Weidman
Dancers in Charles Weidman's *Quest*.

the exercises and movement principles of François Delsarte (1811–
1871), a French scientist of movement and its meanings. Delsarte
was not a dancer—his students and dancers of a later era were
responsible for the application of his laws of movement to dance—
but he knew how to *look* at movement, to observe it, to study it and
to deduce from it the nature of a character and that character's
reaction to environment, stress, emotional experience and the like.
Delsarte, an opera tenor who had lost his voice through bad training,
turned to the study of natural movement. As an outraged observer of
operatic acting, stock gesture and unnatural pantomime, he sought
to discover movement truths. He watched the old and the young, the
rich, the poor, the imprisoned and the free, the ill, the angry, the
fearful, the desperate, the hopeful, the transfigured.

His intensive studies of human behavior in terms of movement led
him to believe that movements emanating from the hips down were
primarily physical; from hips to shoulders, emotional; from shoulders upward, spiritual-mental. The space areas lying outside those
designated segments of the body partook of the same qualities. Thus
it could be said that hands resting on thighs mirror the physical, the

80

Doris Humphrey, Charles Weidman in *Decade*.

sensual, the sexual; those same hands, pressed to the breast, reflect the emotional; hands raised upward to the head, thought or contemplation; and above the head, aspiration.

Duncan refers briefly to her own Delsarte background in an interview made as far back as 1896. St. Denis, in her writings and lectures, frequently referred to Delsarte exercises (including those for breathing) and wrote that one of her major influences was a dance performance by Genevieve Stebbins, a pupil of Delsarte himself, which she had attended as a child. Ted Shawn, shortly before he met, married and partnered St. Denis, took some private instruction in meaningful movement and gesture from Mary Perry King. The name Delsarte was never mentioned, and it was not until Shawn later studied Delsarte methods that he realized Mrs. King's classes were Delsarte-derived. With Mrs. Richard Hovey, a pupil of Delsarte's son, Gustave, Shawn engaged in intensive Delsarte training and, ultimately, introduced Delsarte principles, adapted to dance, into the Denishawn schools. Thus Martha Graham, Doris Humphrey and Charles Weidman, who were to become the leaders in the modern-dance movement a decade later, were Delsarteindoctrinated during their own formative years as Denishawn dancers.

The Delsarte factor, at first glance, might seem peripheral to the purpose of this book. It is not. It is an integral part of an evolving American dance process which has long demanded that choreographers and dancers go below the surface attractions of the human body in movement and probe the meanings of movement. If dancers demand more of dance than superficial attributes and accomplishments, it follows that audiences are going to have to look beyond the outer layers of dance action if they are to savor, to the fullest, the inherent richness of dance itself.

Denishawn contributed immeasurably to this new, or renewed, concept of dance and helped in the building of a public that would, in some measure, take dance seriously. The rebels against Denishawn went even farther and demanded more of their audiences. Entertainment was almost a dirty word.

Isadora, with her innovative ideas, had danced nonetheless to the world's finest classical music. Although this outraged musical purists, the music itself provided critics, music connoisseurs and the public with clues on how to look at her approach to dance. She was, in essence, an extension of that music into substance, into a physicality observable in space.

St. Denis and Shawn clothed their revolutionary ideas in theater dress. There were gorgeous costumes, stunning scenery and dramatic themes. The casual viewer did not have to understand the aesthetic, philosophical and spiritual purposes of the Denishawn dances in order to enjoy himself; looking at the productions—the Babylonian *Ishtar,* reproducing the interior of a vast temple, and the American Indian *The Feather of the Dawn,* reproducing a pueblo on stage, were exciting enough for anyone.

Martha Graham, who left Denishawn in 1923—she had joined the

Hanya Holm.

82

company in 1916—and Doris Humphrey and Charles Weidman, who departed Denishawn in 1928, rebelled against the dance's reliance on familiar music and on its use of opulent sets and costumes, exotic backgrounds and story themes. Graham, Humphrey and Weidman, in company with the independent Helen Tamiris, and Hanya Holm stripped the dance bare. This made it tough going for audiences. Martha Graham, who had built up a national following as an exotic Aztec heroine, a lovely Moorish dancing girl, a fiery Señorita and a lissome Hindu maiden, was suddenly seen in jersey tubing or the equivalent, arms and legs in

Gerda Peterich

Helen Tamiris in *Walt Whitman Suite*.

distorted, angular positions, an expressionless face, and all of it with music that sounded strange or strident or cacophonous or all three.

Doris Humphrey, who had been Ruth St. Denis's special protégée, forsook her repertory of delectable Oriental solos and discarded those music visualizations that had presented her lithe form in a filmy dress with her glinting reddish hair streaming behind her. She stood, instead, in front of a mirror and experimented with falling off-balance. How far could she tip or tilt without crashing to the floor, or without making some sort of recovery by twisting her body in another direction or putting out a foot to stay her fall? She referred to the aesthetic disease afflicting—or so she felt—Denishawn as the "eses," for she said she was sick and tired of being Chinese, Javanese, Japanese, Burmese and the other "eses," and wanted to find out how a woman from Oak Park, Illinois, should dance.

What Doris Humphrey was doing in front of her mirror was experimenting with the pull, or attraction, of gravity. Standing still in accepted verticality or lying flat on the floor were, for her, two poles of *inaction—action* existed along the pathway between the two. She called it, rather dramatically, "the arc between two deaths." What Humphrey saw in this arc, and what she wanted audiences to look for, was a new awareness of gravity as a remarkable tool of dance, of theater, even of thought. On the purely physical side of it, she saw that the farther the body leaned away from uprightness, the more suspenseful, literally and kinetically, the movement became. As the body reached a point of no return as it accelerated along the arc, the more perilous the situation became. The onlooker would catch his breath. Can the dancer recover? Will the dancer crash? Is there any way out?

She was concerned with relating the physical excitement inherent in her concept of this great arc of movement with the suspense of a narrative; with the danger of traveling from like to love to blind passion; with the daring of a thought that departs from the known and reaches out to the untried with the goal being discovery or death, the triumph of genius or . . . a descent to madness. There was no need, of course, for the public to learn about this movement principle of "fall and recovery"—that was something that only she as a choreographer, her students and the Humphrey-Weidman dancers themselves need know. The public need only look at the dance accomplishments evolving from this technical principle.

Modern dance—Martha Graham's *Frescoes,*
based on Egyptian themes (Peggy Lyman, solo,
and Christine Dakin, Charles Brown).

A dance of social protest— Kurt Jooss's
The Green Table (José Limón Dance Company).

Modern dancers of the 1920s and 1930s were not in the mood to compromise. They wanted and needed audiences, but they refused to pamper them. Modern dance was described as "stark," "distorted," "angular," "the cult of ugliness." Hardly inviting prospects for box-office sales. Many of them said, "I don't care if audiences get angry, just as long as they react." Said Graham, "I'll dance as long as anyone comes to see me." Tamiris, a political militant, took up the battle against fascism, as represented by the Spanish Civil War of the 1930s, in a dance called *Adelante.* Her historic *How Long Brethren,* a dance work funded by the Federal Dance Project (a division of the Works Progress Administration that functioned during the Great Depression), was the first major dance by a major choreographer to protest inequities visited upon American blacks.

Other choreographers in the field of modern dance joined a powerful wave of choreographic activity that filled the stages and studio-theaters with statements of social protest conceived in movement terms. Weidman, in his suite titled *Atavisms,* offered an episode called "Lynchtown." Here was a bitter, biting indictment of communal crime in which Americans were victims of Americans. Weidman did not reproduce a lynching on stage, for this was not a dance documentary of a specific murder. Instead, one saw townsfolk responding to a lynching, and they responded not with horror but with excitement, curiosity, eagerness, even pleasure. A mother holds up a child so that he won't miss the killing. Yes, it was, and remains, a horror story, not in the depiction of a crime but in revealing the savagery and moral corruption of some Americans.

Kurt Jooss, in one of the greatest dances of social comment ever created, *The Green Table,* took for his theme the recurring, worldwide crime of war, in which death is the only victor. The ballet—for its movement vocabulary included some elementary ballet steps fused with modern-dance movements—was created in 1932 and won first prize in the first choreographic competition held in Paris by Les Archives Internationales de la Danse. Jooss, a German, had intended to enter the competition with a solo based upon the Medieval Dance of Death. A newspaper story about a speech given by someone named Adolf Hitler struck him with such force that he abandoned medieval death fantasies for the real death he saw coming. *The Green Table,* with a piano score by Frederick Cohen, was created in a matter of days. A half-century later, it retains its power when performed in dance repertories around the world.

The title of the Jooss work refers to the table around which politicians and diplomats, old and greedy men, gather and plan the wars that will destroy the young, the innocent. Heroes are killed or maimed, lovers separated, homes destroyed, and the old seek release in the welcoming arms of death. And when it is all over, the diplomats and politicians reassemble to plan another war.

The Green Table served as the cornerstone of the repertory of the Jooss Ballet for many years. And although the Jooss Ballet company itself disbanded after World War II, *The Green Table* never disappeared entirely and in the 1970s achieved new status in repertories in the United States and abroad. Obviously it is not a pleasant work of theater, with its principal character the remorseless figure of Death, but today's dance audiences know how to look for something in dance that their predecessors did not: a theater piece that would shatter complacency, disturb the emotions, challenge the mind.

5 Ballet and Modern

Ritual in dance—*Sanctus*—
(Michael Onstad), Ballet West.

in Tandem

The aims of modern dance and those of ballet seem to be worlds apart. The modern-dance exponent, both dancer and choreographer, of the twenties, thirties and even into the forties was uncompromising in the pursuit of new artistic goals. Such goals might possibly concern themes of social comment or psychological analysis or biting political commentary. But more than that, even if the modern dancer were dealing with less serious matters, the dancer of this new school was not present to display physical skills, to engage in decorative action in decorative surroundings or, in a word, to "entertain." Entertainment for the sake of diversion played no part in early modern dance. The dancer danced because he had something to say through movement, and a viewer was present because he was interested in what the dancer had to say. This was not a dance of fun and games. Ballet, on the other hand, although it could and did deal with serious themes, weighty matters and controversial collaborations of avant-garde artists, never forswore "theater," with its strong elements of decorativeness, visual attractions, physical prowess . . . entertainment.

One would have every reason to believe that the two forms would never meet, never find a common bond. As we have already noted, John Martin, the great pioneering dance critic of *The New York Times,* described ballet as "spectacular dance" and modern as "expressional dance." The distinctly different purposes of the two forms appeared to preclude any union. It did not.

The dichotomy between ballet and modern dance once ranged from the militant to the belligerent to the destructive. Even such ballet reformers as Michel Fokine, who had rebelled against the strictures of nineteenth-century ballet, dismissed modern dance with the most scathing of comments. Martha Graham attacked ballet publicly. The two, Graham and Fokine, actually had a celebrated confrontation during a question-and-answer period at a lecture. Young modern dancers were forbidden by their employers to attend ballet classes on pain of dismissal. And young ballet students simply laughed at the notion that they could gain anything at all from modern-dance instruction.

In the late 1930s, few people thought that ballet and modern dance would eventually find a meeting ground. Yet there were a few

experiments in the "art" dance of the 1930s that indicated otherwise. In 1933, for example, Ted Shawn founded his company of
men dancers. Most of the eight young men had been college athletes
and their dance training with Shawn was primarily nonballetic, but
there was a touch of what might be called "free-style" ballet, done
in bare feet and without exaggerated turnout of the limbs, included
in classroom exercises.

For the most part, Shawn trained his men through rhythmic
gymnastic exercises, studies in tension and relaxation evolved from
the modern-dance technique of Germany's Mary Wigman, a good
many exercises (parallelisms, oppositions, successions) rooted in
Delsarte principles and, of course, strong ethnic dances borrowed
from cultures in which the male dancer was paramount. But Shawn
himself had long before tossed together a potpourri of virtuosic ballet
actions, done barefoot, as a sort of warmup study. In 1931 while on
tour in Germany, he was pressed for a "light" solo to conclude the
first half of an otherwise serious concert-dance program. Reluctantly
he agreed to perform this study, now titled *Frohsinn*, and surprised
himself by having it emerge as a rousing hit and even hailed by
serious modern-dance followers as an introduction to "the dance of
the future."

Later in the most significant of his creations for his male ensemble,
Kinetic Molpai, he used certain adapted ballet steps for the rousing
apotheosis, the closing celebration, of this masterwork, which found
its ancient heritage in the dances of the threshing floor of ancient
Greece and its theme in the elements of love, conflict, death and that
which lies beyond death. Shawn, in a solo section, actually
executed ballet's whipping *fouettés* barefoot! But was this tour de
force, usually associated with the ballerina as she spins on *pointe*,
actually so remote from the whirling dervish who spins into circular

Ballet of social comment—
Kenneth MacMillan's *Gloria*,
Jennifer Penny, Wayne Eagling
(Royal Ballet).

92

Dramatic movement—Tudor's *Lilac Garden*
with Bruhn and Kirkland (American Ballet Theatre).

orbit when motivated by spiritual ecstasy?

In his historic experiments with "symphonic ballets" in the 1930s, the Ballet Russe's Léonide Massine frequently departed from the traditional movement vocabulary of classical ballet. Never, however, was a departure more noticeable and more influential than that made in the second movement of his *Choreartium,* set to the Brahms Symphony No. 4. Here an ensemble of robed women, bent and bowed as if participants in a great processional of mourning, dominated the scene while the solo figure (Nina Verchinina) served as a focal point with free, expressive movements that had little if anything to do with ballet.

In England in the mid-1930s, Antony Tudor launched a choreographic career that was to take him not only to international recognition as one of the great choreographers of the century, but also to an aesthetic achievement which saw a comfortable union, on several levels, of ballet and modern dance. Tudor's creative output has remained within the field of ballet; the dancers in his works are always ballet-trained; as a teacher, he is a ballet master. But while his basic discipline is that of classical ballet, he employs the expressional principles of modern dance to achieve depth of characterization, intensity of mood and emotional and dramatic stress. So it is that his *Lilac Garden* (*Jardin aux Lilas,* as it is frequently titled) and his *Dark Elegies,* both created in the 1930s, are in the vanguard of those ballets that replace traditional mime with dramatic movement, that use the toe shoe for dramatic accent rather than for technical display, that integrate movements of the torso with balletic action.

Agnes de Mille, also starting in the 1930s but making her first major impacts in the next decade, strayed even farther from ballet technique while working in the ballet field. In her *Three Virgins and a Devil* (1941), not one of the virgins performs on *pointe,* although the Devil includes balletic virtuosity (especially fast turns) in a dance characterization that is basically conceived as comic-dramatic action. The principal virgin (described as the Priggish One) uses a great deal of pelvic action throughout her major solo in accents inconceivable in classical ballet.

De Mille's now-historic *Rodeo* (1942) is not so much nonballetic or modern-dance-influenced as it is just plain dance à la de Mille. There is no *pointe* work in it, but there are all kinds of American folk-dance measures, comic pantomime, tap dancing and, most important, danced acting: Through the prancing steps of open legs seemingly astraddle, she has made horse and rider a single dance figure. In Eugene Loring's *Billy the Kid* (1938), a similar horse-and-rider movement motif is employed, but Loring includes multiple *pirouettes* and *tours en l'air* for Billy, although they are used not for technical display, but as stylized manifestations of the western gunman's bravado. The ballet, in a dream sequence, contains a quite classical *pas de deux* for Billy and his Mexican sweetheart, although the duet itself is seamlessly united with movements indicative of a lurking, watchful, gun-toting outlaw. The great

A mix of ballet, modern and pantomime—Agnes de Mille's *Three Virgins and a Devil*—the late Yurek Lazovsky as the Devil, de Mille (the Priggish Virgin), Ruth Mayer as the Greedy Virgin, Hilda Morales as the Lustful Virgin (American Ballet Theatre).

processionals of humanity which open and close *Billy the Kid* in patterns depicting a trek, an ongoing stream of people ever on the move westward, also weld together the *pirouettes* and air turns of classical ballet with strides, with trudging steps, with knee falls.

Hanya Holm, the modern-dance pioneer who had come to America from Germany in 1931, was especially admired as a teacher. Her own concert group was expertly trained and performed nationwide (1936–1942) with considerable success. In 1941 Holm introduced in her studio a special class for ballet dancers. She was not going to turn them into modern dancers but rather give them

movement principles that would enhance their prowess and their expressive needs in ballet. Among the ballet dancers taking this brief, concentrated course was Donald Saddler. Although he ultimately gained fame as a choreographer for Broadway shows, Italian musicals, revues and television, his choreography for ballet made use of modern-dance principles rather than ballet steps. In such danced dramas of the 1950s as *This Property Is Condemned* (based on the Tennessee Williams play) and *Winesburg, Ohio* (Robert Sherwood), he used "gut feeling" to determine the movements for character, and situation determined steps, gesture, action.

Valerie Bettis, a member of Hanya Holm's concert-dance group, not only moved from concert dance to musical comedy as a dancer, but she was one of the first modern dancers to choreograph a ballet for a ballet company. In 1947 she created *Virginia Sampler* for the American-based Ballet Russe de Monte Carlo, and in 1952 she turned Tennessee Williams's enormously popular *A Streetcar Named Desire* into a ballet for the Slavenska-Franklin company. Although both contained ballet steps, the salient feature was action born of situation and role, not so much modern dance in technique as modern dance in matters of freely invented movements.

The problem of how to look at a given dance or dancer was summarized, in almost ironic fashion, by Bettis herself in two closely related dances presented under widely different environmental conditions. In 1943 for her first concert in New York, she created and performed *The Desperate Heart,* accompanied by a poem she had commissioned from John Malcolm Brinnin. It was, and remains, a dance remarkable for its power, for guiding, but not pushing, the viewer into an inner life of loneliness and desperation and, finally, of resignation. It attracted only the small public that existed for modern dance in those days.

Five years after *The Desperate Heart* was first performed, Bettis went into her first Broadway musical, *Inside U.S.A.,* in which she captivated audiences with her sizzling dance scene as Tiger Lily and conquered audiences in a dance called *The Haunted Heart,* both highlights of a show choreographed by the modern-dance pioneer, Helen Tamiris. *Haunted Heart* and *Desperate Heart* were dances on exactly the same theme and were performed by a modern dancer using modern-dance technique. *But* the audience that adored *The Haunted Heart* at the Ziegfeld Theater would most certainly have complained of total mystification at a concert performance of *The Desperate Heart.* Why? Because the majority of theatergoers would maintain that they cannot possibly understand wordless dance about some kind of neurotic ailment, but that same public would be absolutely confident that a producer of a musical would not give them something they could not understand. In other words, take a facsimile of *Desperate Heart,* call it a blues routine, put it in a show and you have a hit! Ah, packaging!

Sometimes the ballet-modern dance route was reversed. Todd Bolender, dancer-choreographer with George Balanchine's New York City Ballet, in 1955 created what was to become his best-known ballet, *The Still Point*, for a modern-dance group, the Dance Drama Company, headed by Emily Frankel (a dancer with the old Humphrey-Weidman company) and Mark Ryder (of the Martha Graham Dance Company). Frankel and Ryder danced the leads. *Pointe* shoes of course were not used. The next year Bolender revised his work to include the *pointe*, and it was presented by the New York City Ballet with Melissa Hayden and Jacques d'Amboise as its stars.

John Butler, who had danced principal roles with Graham and had headed his own modern-dance troupe, was invited to create ballets for ballet companies. In most instances his works remained close to modern-dance techniques, heightened for virtuosic effects by adapted ballet actions. One of his featured dancers, Glen Tetley, went much, much farther toward closing the gap between ballet and modern dance. First, as a dancer he made the transition from a brilliant exponent of modern dance (with Holm, Graham, Butler) to a highly skilled ballet performer capable of dancing classical roles, even those in the lyrical-romantic style so definitively performed by Erik Bruhn. Eventually his choreographic essays moved away from pure modern-dance expression into the field of ballet, where he was able to build a successful career, particularly in Europe, as the creator of "modern" ballets in which highly flexible torsos, gravity responses, abstract themes and avant-garde music were interrelated with certain balletic feats.

Bruce Marks's career has taken him from child dancer and teenage principal with Pearl Lang and her modern-dance groups to *premier danseur* in such classics as *Swan Lake* with the American Ballet Theatre. In the 1970s he became an exponent of the classical style of Denmark's nineteenth-century August Bournonville during a brief period with the Royal Danish Ballet. The directorship of Ballet West, a national company with headquarters in Salt Lake City, Utah, was given him in 1976. He has choreographed ballets both at home and abroad that make equal use of his modern-dance and ballet backgrounds.

The overlapping and interrelating of two differing approaches to dance is of interest here not so much because of the resulting stage products as in the revelations of changing attitudes and tastes with respect to dance itself. Modern choreographers working in the ballet milieu would not have had a chance at success if the public had not become prepared, at least in some measure, to take dance seriously

as far as theme, psychological probings, intellectual challenges were concerned.

Audiences, at first, were not always willing to look at dance with an eye toward being aesthetically or intellectually challenged. It was easier to lose oneself in a fairy tale or to respond with gasps of incredulity at feats of skill. Still, there were those—and by the 1940s their numbers were increasing—who realized that there were emotional rewards to be found in Tudor's *Pillar of Fire,* with its heroine a spinster in search of emotional as well as physical fulfillment. Later, in 1950, there was an audience for Jerome

Acting-dancing—Eugene Loring's
Billy the Kid with
Joseph Clark as Billy, John Hiatt
as Pat Garrett (Ballet West).

Robbins's *The Age of Anxiety* (based on the W. H. Auden poem), a ballet as cheerless as its title suggests, but a dance work that would address itself to a state of mind besetting a nation.

Put in the most extreme categories, *think* and *non-think* ballets provided a choice for the dancegoer. The best of the *think* ballets were absorbing, dramatic, sometimes exciting, usually stirring, as well as being challenging and disturbing. If one wanted dance frills and thrills, a Bolshoi Ballet Highlights program with multiple spins, vaulting leaps, split-second hurtlings and daring catches wouldn't tax the mind one whit. Fun! Or one might wish to see Balanchine's first made-in-America ballet, *Serenade* (1934), in which the turns were gentler, the leaps softer, the lifts and catches delicately suspenseful and the whole a cornucopia of movement images so beautiful, so fresh, so radiant that they would stay in the mind forever. Looking at the dance, in those now distant thirties, forties and fifties, viewers had embarked upon a maturing process that would lead to greater scope for choreographers and, more important, new and exciting horizons for the dance public.

But even in the early 1980s, audiences were not always prepared to see what ballet had to offer in nondiversionary areas. These audiences were not so much misled as they were unprepared. As an example, during a season by Britain's Royal Ballet at New York's vast Metropolitan Opera House, there were occasions when obviously disgruntled audience members got up and left during performances of three contemporary ballets. They had come to see a real, live prince (Prince Charles), who had been present at a gala as the season started, and, at subsequent performances, these unthinking, unknowledgeable people who had paid up to thirty-five dollars for a single ticket expected to see more princes, as well as princesses and all sorts of royal characters and happenings, on stage at all presentations.

These attendants at the ballet, who had misled themselves, were happy enough with the Royal Ballet's *The Sleeping Beauty* and *Swan Lake*—both contained dull passages, but the classics may be forgiven for being dull in spots if they are grand about it—but they didn't at all like a very sophisticated ballet with no plot and no princes and set to a dry Stravinsky score (*Scènes de Ballet* by Ashton), and they certainly weren't amused by the commentary on and tribute to the British dead of World War I in Kenneth MacMillan's *Gloria*. Members of this audience assumed that ballet was just one thing— royal fun—when, in truth, it ranges from Grimm (fantasy) to grim (realism).

Professor Samuel Selden of the drama department of the University of North Carolina once told his drama majors that the performing arts could work on three levels: They could divert, they could stimulate, they could illumine. One was not more important than the other—although to illumine a heart and mind was the rarest—but that each served a different function. With the dance explosion in America in the 1970s and 1980s, a vast new dance public had to discover what it was looking at in order to find out what it was looking for—diversion, stimulation, illumination. All *are* still there. The choice is ours and the search for the best in each of these three areas constitutes *our* adventure.

Characterization in
classic ballet—*Swan Lake*—
Ludmila Semenyaka as Odette
(Bolshoi Ballet).

6 Jazz

Movements in jazz style with Bob Fosse.

Jack Cole, stripped to the waist and his torso gleaming with oil, jumped from the top of the short flight of steps leading to the dance floor, landed on his knees and slid up to a ringside table of diners in the old Rainbow Room atop Rockefeller Center. A woman, with a few martinis under her belt, looked down at this muscled creature in provocative backbend at her knees, let out a "Jesus Christ!" and fainted.

Cole, in his many engagements at the Rainbow Room, New York's elegant and high-toned supper club, and other classy night spots, was introducing a wholly new kind of jazz dance to the American public. His own dance background was neither as a tap dancer nor as a contestant in the jazz sections of the old Harvest Moon Ball. He had been a pupil of Ruth St. Denis and Ted Shawn, had danced in their companies, learned St. Denis's Oriental-style movements and Ted Shawn's contemporary dance expositions of Negro spirituals. But he was living in a jazz age. So, in the late 1930s and throughout the 1940s, he decided to recast what he knew into a jazz rhythm and style that was to be Jack Cole jazz.

This was the age of swingtime. Cole, augmenting his knowledge of Oriental dance with lessons in authentic Hindu *mudras* (hand gestures) from the great American ethnic-dance expert, La Meri, startled and enchanted show business with his Hindu dance in swing. He also journeyed to Harlem, but instead of learning tap or the Lindy or the like, he took the rhythms of Harlem and fused them with his modern-dance technique—the fainting lady at the Rainbow Room attested to the effectiveness of his ventures. His success as a jazz dancer of concert-dance caliber took him not only into the posh nightclubs, but, as a choreographer, into movies and musical comedy. Imitators sprang up everywhere, but Jack Cole and his associate dancers—Anna Austin and Florence Lessing being special favorites with Cole himself and with the public—were tops.

When he "swung" East Indian dance, the elegance as well as the mystery of the Orient were in his deportment and in his gestures, but the contemporary rhythms and accents gave these dances a new sensuality (even sexuality) and chic ribaldry that the public adored. Jack knew his *mudras* well and, with this gesture language, could express himself succinctly. Since he was vastly temperamental,

Movements in jazz style with Bob Fosse.

easily annoyed, impatient with anything short of perfection, he would not only scream at recalcitrant orchestra leaders and managers, but he would also curse, in Hindu gesture, an audience member who was too busy drinking or eating or talking to pay proper attention. On one such occasion, Ruth St. Denis, who was sitting at a table with me, noticed Jack's fingers, eyebrows and nostril flarings flying out from his performance. She said, "Oh, my! What Jack just said to that inebriated lady doesn't bear translation into words!"

For art purists jazzing up the ancient classical dance of India or

Ballroom disco.

introducing jazz rhythms into the Western world's classical ballet seemed almost sacrilegious. Yet the popular dances of ordinary people, their music, their crafts, have always fed and kept alive the professional artists and the art expressions of nations and cultures. For this century jazz and its derivatives constitute the rhythmic base not only for much of our music but also for our theatrical dance, our so-called art dances.

In the 1930s concert-dance artists looked at any sort of jazz-rooted dance as suitable only for vaudeville, stage shows, nightclubs. This era, of course, was pretelevision, and since radio was the mass medium of communications and entertainment, and since radio could not provide visuals, there was no popular pressure exerted upon dancers and choreographers to incorporate jazz into their work. Ted Shawn, for example, thought of jazz as a decadent expression that was an aftermath to the debilitating experience of World War I. Isadora Duncan, in 1927, wrote, "It seems to me monstrous for anyone to believe that Jazz rhythm expresses America. Jazz rhythm expresses the South African savage." Speaking of the popular dances of her day, she said, "Their movements are choppy, end-stopped, abrupt. They lack the continuing beauty of the curve. They are satisfied with being the points of angles which spur on the nerves. The music of today, too, only makes the nerves dance. Deep emotion, spiritual gravity, are entirely lacking. We dance with the jerky gestures of puppets."

St. Denis felt similarly about jazz. But late in her career, when she was in her eighties, she appeared on a program with Alvin Ailey who, with Carmen de Lavallade, was dancing *Roots of the Blues*. She watched from the wings every time they danced, and at the end of the engagement, she went to Ailey and said, "Now, through you, I understand jazz. You showed me not only its roots but its heart."

To these oldtime pioneers and, indeed, to balletomanes and those who took modern dance seriously, jazz music and jazz dance belonged to the field of tap, to the Savoy Ballroom in Harlem, to the dance floor in clubs or around juke boxes. It didn't seem to have much to do with the art of dance.

Then in the 1940s Jerome Robbins came up with his first smashingly successful ballet, *Fancy Free*, followed by *Interplay* (done first in a musical before being transferred to ballet repertory) and other works. These were instant hits with the public, but there remained a hard "corps" of Russian-ballet-rooted fans and experts

A Tharp rehearsal
(*Chapters and Verses*).

Movements in modern dance with
Twyla Tharp and Richard
Colton in *Baker's Dozen*.

who believed that jazz dancing had no business in ballet, that it was a corrupting influence. None of them had stopped to consider that a century earlier Denmark's August Bournonville had placed a rousing *tarantella* in the midst of his ballet choreography for *Napoli*, that Fanny Elssler and her contemporaries took dances of Spain or Lithuania or some other land and balleticized them, and, even more pertinent, that Marius Petipa introduced national dances, the then popular social dances of various peoples, into such classics as *Swan Lake*. The jazz dances of our century were no more alien to ballet than were the *mazurka*, the *czardas*, the *jota* of Petipa's day.

Jazz-dance drama—John
Butler's *Portrait of Billie*
with Carmen de Lavallade
and Ulysses Dove
(Alvin Ailey American
Dance Theater).

Choreographically Robbins went a step beyond *Swan Lake,* in which national dances were edited and theatricalized but not translated into ballet technique. He mixed *tours en l'air, pirouettes* and the like with *snakehips,* a bump and a grind, a touch of the old soft shoe, social dance steps. It was a job of fusion and it worked like a charm. Audiences could look for the same technical exactitude and physical prowess characteristic of classical ballet technique, but they would have to accept it and savor it in new dress. A skirt might replace a *tutu,* and a rumba might swivel-hip the usually vertical stance of the ballet dancer's customary style, but the result was still

ballet.

It was often said that the popular jitterbugging of the time mirrored the fact that post-World War II America had the jitters, was cursed with the nervousness that offended Isadora's aesthetic tastes, but whatever the reasons, jazz represented the times, and if ballet and modern dance and ethnic art dance were to be a part of the age itself, then the rhythms of that age, nerves and all, could not be omitted. Yes, the classics would remain and new dances could eschew jazz entirely, but somewhere in repertories the popular beat of the thirties, forties and fifties had to be seen as well as heard.

Actually there is no such thing as a jazz-dance technique. What one finds are techniques—ballet, modern, ethnic, tap, etc.—invested with jazz rhythms and clothed in jazz style. Many of the foremost jazz-dance teachers in the United States, Canada and Western Europe start their classes with a ballet *barre*—that is, the standard exercises of classical ballet done at the start of a ballet class. Some teachers use a modern-dance base and begin classes with a partial modern-dance warmup of stretches to loosen the body.

Looseness, in fact, is an essential characteristic of jazz dance. Hips, shoulders, wrists and ankles should be free to engage in that loose-limbed, carefree, seemingly improvisational action that give jazz dancing its special insouciance. Watching the jazz dancer, one looks especially for a command of "isolations." This simply means that the jazz dancer can seemingly send a hip flying in one direction, a shoulder in another, a foot in yet another, while a hand, rotating on the wrist, might appear to have a life all its own.

The ballet dancer, although the trunk must be mobile, tends to keep the body in control as a unit, with arms and legs moving in the same direction and with hips tucked under. The modern dancer makes use of isolations, but these are controlled by, say, Graham-style contractions and releases or by some other modern-dance discipline. The jazz dancer's isolations mirror a freed body, the free action of improvisation, the free embroideries of musical syncopation, the impulses of the instant.

Tap, however, is the technique most often associated with jazz. Jazz had its inception as a musical expression. Music lives through sound. The tap dancer's forte is in the intricacies of the sounds he can produce. Hence jazz and tap have common, or related, roots. The tap dancer existed long before there was jazz, a musical form

A modern-dance jazz solo—
Ailey's *Cry* with Donna Wood.

A modern-dance jazz solo—
Ailey's *Cry* with Donna Wood.

The birth of jazz—Donald McKayle's
District Storyville with Donna Wood
and Marilyn Banks (Alvin Ailey
American Dance Theater).

emanating from New Orleans about the beginning of this century. Black artists were the originators of it as they were the inventors of "step" dances, destined to evolve into tap, a century before. Thus through the black performer, jazz and tap found easy union.

When jazz dance extended its areas of action beyond the field of tap, something new was added. With tap the jazz rhythm was centered in the feet. With ballet, modern dance and other techniques, jazz pervaded the entire body. There was no single center, so the principle of "polycentrism"—the concept of many centers— was introduced. Thus rhythmic interest could be shifted swiftly,

amusingly, sensually, sexually or just plain delightfully to any part of the body. The hips, next then to the feet, were probably the most obvious focal point of jazz when it explored beyond tap.

A jazz dance that concentrated on the hips was called the *shimmy*. It was invented (or devised as a stage routine), very probably, by a vaudeville dancer named Gilda Gray, who achieved her peak of stardom in the early 1920s. Whether or not she was the first to use high-speed shaking, shivering, shimmying hips is arguable, but certainly the *shimmy* became her trademark. The classical ballerina, Alicia Markova, surprised English balletomanes when in the 1930s she let her hips go jazzily astray in a movement described as "snakehips" in a ballet called *High Yellow*. Twenty years later the great American black dancer, Katherine Dunham, featured a dance called "Florida Swamp Shimmy" in a production that she choreographed and staged, in *Le Jazz Hot*. And in the earliest days of this century, a performer named Perry Bradford, famed for a number called "Bullfrog Hop," urged all who would listen: "First you commence to wiggle from side to side, Get 'way back and do the Jazzbo Glide, Then you do the shimmy with plenty of pep, Stoop low, yeah Bo', and watch your step." But the *shimmy* and its loose-hipped relatives existed as black dance expressions well before Gilda Gray, Mae West (who also claimed she invented it) and other white entertainers had brought it to the legitimate theater.

Jazz dance and jazz music spread from New Orleans to Harlem in New York City to other black centers, and soon changed the course of white culture and, indeed, affected the world's tastes with respect to popular music. Oldtime hoofers like Bert Williams, a dazzling black dance star of the Gay Nineties and well into this century, took his audience from the days of the *cakewalk* to the era of *strut, shuffle* and *grind,* dances whose titles are pretty much self-explanatory.

Williams, and such great tap-jazz dance successors as Bill ("Bojangles") Robinson, Buck and Bubbles, the Nicholas Brothers, and later greats like Honi Coles and Sandman Sims, are the artists who have made jazz dance in tap form an American classic. Choreographers for Broadways shows, television, ballet and modern dance have kept the jazz base of these masters, but have moved on into a variety of forms. Donald McKayle tells the story of the birth of jazz in his modern-dance creation, *District Storyville;* Alvin Ailey, for his own Alvin Ailey American Dance Theater, has taken one of Bert Williams's favorite dance styles and made a full dance-theater

Jazz ballet—Jerome Robbins—*Fancy Free* with
Buddy Balough as one of the sailors
(American Ballet Theatre).

Song-dance-show biz in Ailey's *The Mooche*
to music of Duke Ellington with Sarita Allen.

piece of it, *The Mooche*; and once Jerome Robbins had experimented with balleticized jazz in both *Fancy Free* and *Interplay*, he created a signature ballet for the late 1950s called *N. Y. Export, Op. Jazz* to a commissioned jazz-dance score by Robert Prince. England's Frederick Ashton gave the Royal Ballet his *Jazz Calendar* (1968), and two years later Russian-born George Balanchine created *Who Cares?* to the music of George Gershwin for his New York City Ballet.

How to look at jazz dancing? Well, if it is contained within tap, the tip is to listen as well as look. If a choreographer has chosen to use elements of jazz in balletic form or for a modern-dance piece, is the jazz idiom superimposed, or is it integrated with the choreographer's own movement vocabulary to achieve a new kind of expression? Surely one savors those "isolations" which constitute rhythmic-anatomical surprises to delight the eye and the senses. For the senses are absolutely essential to an appreciation of jazz . . . senses as "antennae" for feelings. The late Marshall Stearns, perhaps our greatest expert on jazz dance, its origins, phases and accomplishments, described it best when he wrote, "The characteristic that distinguishes American vernacular dance—as it does jazz music—is *swing,* which can be heard, felt and seen, but defined only with great difficulty." So, FEEL THE SWING!

7   Ethnic Dance

The dance of India—Kathakali dancers.

La Meri, born Russell Meriwether Hughes in Kentucky and raised in Texas, by 1940 had become one of the world's major authorities on ethnic dance. She had gone from dancing Mexican, Spanish and ballet numbers in vaudeville to in-depth studies of the ancient and contemporary art dances of a variety of cultures from Spain to India, from North Africa to Hawaii. Her travels took her to remote villages, great temples, obscure cafés, tents in the desert, where she looked, remembered, copied and, in all cases, studied with the dance masters of that area. On her return to America, with the outbreak of World War II, she began to offer programs of ethnic dance in concerts on Broadway and on tour. In order that her audiences would know what to look for, she prefaced her performances with a brief talk-demonstration on the salient features of the dances to be seen.

Long before La Meri, American audiences had been exposed to ethnic dance, but the word "ethnic" had not been used. The preferred term was "exotic." Carnival dancers on the midway had given a gawking public *hootchy-kootchy* displays; Little Egypt held forth at a world's fair; Hawaiian dancers rustled their grass (or cellophane) skirts as they swayed their hips; and one Spanish dancer even clamped her teeth around the back of a chair and spun around in a display of dental fortitude.

On a far higher plane, Ruth St. Denis had used Oriental themes and rich costuming and decor to contain her dance ideas. She did not, however, use authentic ethnic-dance techniques. When Uday Shankar and his company first came to the United States from India in the 1930s, he brought with him theatricalized versions of Indian temple dances, and he clothed his productions with gorgeous costumes. La Meri, although possessing gorgeous costumes, could not afford a big company or lavish productions. She was determined to give the public authentic ethnologic (later shortened to "ethnic") dances, and she was dedicated to explaining their backgrounds and meanings to her viewers.

When La Meri began her campaign, you would not have found the term "ethnic dance" in any dance book or general encyclopedia. Today it is there. Ethnic dance is part of the world of dance.

Looking at ethnic dance is quite different from looking at ballet,

The dance of Bali—temple dancers.

modern dance, tap, or jazz, for you are looking at a people and a people's history. And the more one knows about that history, that culture, the greater the enjoyment. A student of East Indian dance would not dream of trying to learn the intricate steps, the complex hand gestures, the myriad rhythms of *Bharata Natyam* or *Kathakali* (two of the great schools of Indian dance) without knowing something about the Hindu religion, some words in Sanskrit and Hindi and how to wear a sari.

The general audience need not feel that studies in Hindu philosophy are essential to enjoyment of the dances of India—

The dance of Cambodia—
Court Dance: "Mekhala"
(Goddess of the Waters)
and "Ream Eyso"
(Storm Spirit).

although it is helpful to know that Shiva, one of the Hindu trinity of supreme gods, is also Lord of the Dance. For dances of, by and for Shiva abound in the vast repertory of East Indian dance. As for the gesture language of the Hindu dance, La Meri used to come in front of the theater curtain and demonstrate the key gestures in the dances to be shown. The gestures ranged from the imitative—fish, deer, elephant—through the semisymbolic—dawn, night, twinkling stars—to the fully symbolic—inner ecstasy, power, invocation to Shiva. Today's less patient audiences would not accept a lesson before entertainment. Furthermore, today's public has had years of exposure to East Indian dance through later appearances by Uday Shankar, familiarity with Indian music through Ravi Shankar (Uday's popular musician brother), tours by Ram Gopal, Indrani, Ritha Devi, and performances by such expert Indian dance exponents (born in America) as Matteo or Nala Najan. Artists such as Bhaskar and his followers have accented in their programs the virtuosities and theatricalities inherent in Indian dance, thus bringing an appreciation of these ancient dances closer to the action-minded Westerner.

The dances of Indonesia—particularly those of Bali—have been seen, albeit at infrequent intervals, from the 1920s, when Ruth St. Denis, Ted Shawn and their Denishawn Dancers offered Javanese scenes in their programs, through the period of Devi Dja and her Javanese Dancers of the 1930s and 1940s, to the more frequent appearances of dancers from Bali in later years. The Hindu religion and its legends, myths and parables are present here as they are in India, but altered considerably to fit a different, if related, culture. By the time India's dance had filtered down through Indochina to Indonesia, the meanings of the *mudras,* the gestures, had almost disappeared. What remained were the decorative manipulations of the fingers in dance traceries and filigrees of exquisite, delicate

beauty.

Furthermore, the child dancers of Bali were, just for starters, adorable to look at, far more acceptable on first meeting than the more austere, mature dancers of India. Although there are dances in which gestures have little or no meaning to be found in India, and other dances that are sweeping or romantic or simply visually exciting, such as many of those from the *Kathak* (primarily Muslim) and *Manipuri* schools of Indian dance, most of the great classic dances and dance-dramas of India require of the audience concentration, patience and effort. If one is willing to do more than sit back and say, "Show me," the dance of India, with its intricate rhythms, steps and gestures accompanying its complexes of gods and complexity of ideas, can be an enormously rewarding aesthetic experience.

The decorative nature of the dances of Thailand and Cambodia and of the Indonesian islands make them instantly more accessible— hence acceptable—to those who are not familiar with backgrounds of ethnic dance. But these cultures also have dance-dramas that go on for hours—even days—and although battles with demons are always exciting, mythologies also deal with more tranquil moments,

The dance of Spain—lessons for the young
(Tina Ramirez, instructor).

The dance of China—acrobatics; scarf dance; gymnastics.

The dance of Japan—Kabuki dance-drama.

with contemplative periods, and these are not easy for the stranger to follow. Thus most dance stories coming from India through neighboring countries into Indonesia are severely cut and thoroughly edited for export to Western theater.

While traveling either as a tourist to the South Pacific or to the nearest theater at home, the dance follower might easily believe that with Polynesian dances there is little to look for other than the gentle sway of hips accompanied be pleasant arm ripplings. Truth to tell, the Hawaiian hula was originally a sitting dance, and all attention was focused on the hands and arms as they told simple stories of

love and myths and tales of the fearful goddess of the volcano, Pele.

According to La Meri, we can thank Christian missionaries for the hip undulations in the modern hula. Originally the Hawaiian girls sat and told their gesture stories while the men dancers stood and stepped in typical male bravado. The missionaries, shocked at the near nudity of the innocent Hawaiian maidens and having run out of Mother Hubbards with which to clothe the poor pagan creatures, sent off to Tahiti for grass skirts. The Hawaiians dutifully donned the new apparel and, enchanted with the lovely rustle of the grass skirts, got up on their feet for the first time in the history of the hula and moved their hips from side to side in order to rustle more effectively. So in looking at the hula—at least the genuine hula—today, remember to *listen* to the rustle of skirts, but *look* only (or mostly) at the hands and the tales they tell.

The dances of these island peoples, from the comparatively simple ones found in Polynesia to the elaborate rituals of Indonesia, tend to be leisurely. They reflect a way of life in which pressures and need for speed are almost totally absent. Look and relax is the key. Furthermore, many of the dances of Indonesia are rooted in the trance dance, the purpose of which is, through repetition, to throw the doer and the viewer into a trance. Thus if some of these performances seem very long, simply remember that you are neither bored nor sleepy, but rather that you are a participant in a most therapeutic trance dance.

If one can trace the influence of India's dance arts from the Indian subcontinent itself south and east to Indochina, Indonesia and Polynesia, it is also fascinating to pursue another migration in a different direction—westward. Two thousand years ago, restless migrants, many of them expert metalworkers, moved into Persia, Mesopotamia, Egypt. They tarried in Egypt long enough to earn the name by which they are known in many lands—gypsies. Those who traveled from Egypt across North Africa to Spain brought with them the rhythms and airs and attitudes of the Orient filtered through Arab and Moorish cultures. The fruit of these mixtures became—
FLAMENCO.

The popularity of the Oriental-rooted flamenco has obscured, especially with respect to the American public, the remarkable range of Spanish dance. Flamenco, of course, is exciting. It is the gypsies' statement of pride, independence, passion, temperament, fire. The flamenco dancer holds the body not only with the fierce pride of the

The dance of Mexico—Ramón Galindin, Yaqui Indian
deer dance (Ballet Hispánico).

Spaniard but also with the alertness, the wariness of a cat. The speed with which the feet move through the rhythmic intricacies of a *zapateado,* a dance of elaborate heel beats (ranging from the whispering to the shattering), captures both eye and ear. This is usually, but not always, a man's dance. The gypsy flamenco woman has her *alegrías,* which starts with *palmadas,* clapping the hands in a rhythmic statement, and continues with elaborate steps that give exciting motion and life to the long, ruffled train of her dress. The train itself can suggest a proud peacock or it can be made to swirl like foam, to hug the limbs or to trail the body in regal detachment.

Flamenco seems to be improvised, and in gypsy homes, cafés and patios, it is indeed freely invented. For the stage it must be set, at least to a degree. The Spanish "school" dances, so-called because they are taught, are traditional dances that can be learned from teachers. These range from the courtly *pavane* of four centuries ago

The dance of Africa—
National Dance Company of Senegal.

The dance of Africa—the American
Pearl Primus with drummers in an African dance.

through the *fandango* and *bolero* to the *seguidillas* and its modern descendant, the *sevillanas*. These are dances of elegance combined with infectious vitality.

Each of Spain's many regions has its own characteristic dances. The Basques are almost balletic in their dances. Not for them heel beats on the floor; rather, leg beats in the air such as in ballet's *entrechat* or *cabriole*. The *jota* of Aragon (and elsewhere) is really a peasant dance. In ancient days it served as a fertility dance. Performing alongside newly planted fields, the dancers jumped as high as they could in a prayer indicative of the height of the crop to be grown if God looks and listens. Today it is a festival dance for fields, villages and even theaters, where it can serve as a rousing finale to a Spanish dance program.

By contrast a dance of Galicia, the *Muiñeira Gallega*, celebrates in dance the traditional virtues of female modesty and male gallantry

The dance of Armenia—Antranig Armenian Folk Dance Ensemble on Ellis Island with Manhattan in the background.

pictured in dances of courtship. This may start as a dance for two— the maiden's eyes, of course, are demurely downcast while the man is bold—and continue as a group dance including patterns where the men and women dance separately. Some scholars believe this to be a dance of ancient Celtic origins; others see in it, especially in the dancing of the men, echoes of the pyrrhic dances of classical Greece, one of the colonizers of the Iberian peninsula.

The age-old distinctions between the behavior of men and women is reflected in almost all ethnic dances, on the communal folk-dance levels as well as on the ethnic-dance-art level. Nowhere is it more sharply defined in body terms than in Spanish dance. Look and you will notice that although the Spanish woman holds not only her head but her bosom high in pride and independence, the pelvis is modestly retracted. The man, on the other hand, dances with pelvis thrust forward in aggressive maleness. (Doris Humphrey respected all these Spanish male-female characteristics in her modern-dance masterpiece of 1953, *Ritmo Jondo*, created for José Limón and his company.)

Spanish dance, because of its overtness, its pacing, its romantic airs and a highly charged dynamic level, is far more accessible to the responses of an American viewer than, say, the usually serene, leisurely paced, undemonstrative dances of Japan and China. Both cultures, of course, have their lively folk dances, and their folklore allows for dragons and lions and other creatures who come alive through the help of gorgeous masks, splendid wigs and sumptuous costumes. The Chinese are famed for using gymnasts in dance and for rhythmic expositions of martial arts, but their traditional operas, which are more like story ballets, can and do have long stretches of minimal movement and, unedited, continue for hours. But for the patient, for those who savor delicacy of gesture, refinement of step, beauty of stance, the Chinese opera and Japan's *Kabuki* theater, as well as the *Noh* plays, offer the viewer sweet rewards.

In exploring, observing and finding out how best to appreciate ethnic dances, the curious, the adventuresome, could travel the world year after year. But it is now possible to see the world's dances in one's local (or nearby) theaters. Removing a dance from its natural habitat to the Western stage entails some losses and requires skillful adaptations. To see Balinese dancers performing in their temple grounds as Pacific breezes caress one's body is quite different from dashing out of a jammed subway or bus through a crowded theater lobby to be squeezed into a seat from which there seems to be no escape. Thus entrepreneurs of Balinese dance or India's temple dances or the village dances of, say, the Ukraine must select, edit and theatricalize their wares. The "folk," more than the "art," dances require this special treatment.

All dances come from the folk themselves. They have developed over centuries and even millennia as expressions of a nation, a culture, a region, a village, a clan. As folk dances, they are the province of everyone. These are dances to be done, not watched as a performance. But every culture produces the individual with extra ambition, with unique skill, and these "specials" draw from folk materials to make more personal expressions. A priesthood, in its training for rituals, introduces the element of performing. In due course, celebrants become divided into those who do and those who do something special while others watch. The art dances of ethnic cultures have grown from the soil of folk expression to flower in unique ways, art ways.

India, Japan, Spain and other specific cultures have produced art dances as well as folk dances. Others have not. There is nothing at all theatrical about an American square dance. But give it to a

choreographer, such as Agnes de Mille, and you have a high point in a ballet like *Rodeo,* or a key element in a great Broadway musical such as *Oklahoma!*

Most of the dances of the American Indian or the tribal African are communal dances, some recreational but most of religious origin and purpose. There are elements in all that are innately theatrical but only by chance—the great leaps of the towering Watusis of Africa or the intricate hoop dances of the Plains Indians—but if such dances are to be acceptable on stage, they require selection of step and movement to ensure variety and to provide that quality of display essential to professional performing.

India's temple dances, performed by highly trained dancers, are theatrical to begin with. Virtuosity and performing polish are already present. The transfer from temple courtyard to stage is comparatively simple. Haiti boasts some fine folk dances, of African and French origin and combinations thereof, and exciting voodoo rituals, but it has no ethnic-dance art. Or one should say *had* not, for today it does, simply because a highly trained professional dancer named Jean-Léon Destiné took the physical prowesses that emerged from voodoo ceremonies and forged from them a body discipline and

The dance of Appalachian and Southern America—The Vanaver Caravan, at Jacob's Pillow, doing folk dancing and clogging.

training technique that could serve Haitian dance themes, scenes and subjects. This was a manufactured—and successfully so— ethnic-dance art.

The Soviet Union, through ballet-trained folk-dance experts like Igor Moiseyev, has taken its vast wealth of folk dances, shaped them, theatricalized them and given them to ballet-trained professionals to perform in theaters and arenas around the world. More than the folk flavor and colorful folk costumes and zesty folk music are present. Dances such as these are authentic in step, dress, sound and spirit for Uzbekistan or Outer Mongolia or Georgia, but they are not exact replicas of what is done on home turf.

For the viewer to enjoy ethnic dance fully, be it the pure art dances of a people or the theatricalized folk dances of a region, it is wise to look beyond the surface pleasures afforded by a lusty step here, an exotic gesture there. It does not take too much time to pick up a book or pamphlet and find out where these dances came from, who invented them, why they are danced. You and I may never have the world at our feet, but through ethnic dance we can have the feet of the world's peoples—unshod, in moccasins, with spike heels, in leather boots, with bare soles dipped in henna, decorated with thongs or bells, covered in satin, caressed by fur, placed on stilts—in front of us in rhythmic travels through our land and other lands.

8 Show Biz

Modern social dance—
Mary Tyler Moore, Jacques d'Amboise.

Show-business dancing, like show business itself, requires no guidelines for enjoyment. Its very name tells us that the presenters and the performers are in business to show us, the audience, what they can do with light comedy, catchy tunes, a bevy of pretty girls and a batch of handsome boys, bright costumes and scenery, some tricks or surprises to make us gasp, bits of nostalgia to make us sigh, lots of things to make us laugh. Yet it is possible, even with dances directed toward diversion, to derive greater pleasure from them if we know where they came from, what their characteristics are and what special skills are required of the dancers in order for them to entertain us to the fullest.

In show business the most popular dance form is tap. Yes, it has had periods of decline, particularly in the 1940s when ballet and modern dance entered the field of musical comedy as suppliers of a dance vocabulary that would help define characters and advance the plot of the show. But tap never totally disappeared from variety shows, nightclubs, movies. Nor, with the great sweep to popularity of ballet from the 1940s into the 1980s, did it disappear from dance schools around the country. For kids in big cities or little towns, tap retained its position as a nice combination of recreation and discipline for the growing child. It was, and is, an ideal way for boys to get into dance because tap never seemed arty, or possibly effeminate, to fathers who wanted only baseball for their sons. Fred Astaire and Gene Kelly are tap-dance idols to generations of moviegoers and their children. Lynn Swann, one of the great football players, began to develop his movement skills with tap lessons; Richard Cragun, one of the most brilliant of male ballet dancers, started out with tap; for more than half a century, hundreds of Radio City Music Hall Rockettes have earned a good living tapping in matchless unison.

Looking at tap dancing, Americans may take understandable pride in the fact that tap is an American invention. Its origins, curiously, are rooted in the rhythms of Africa and the basic technique of Irish clog dancers. The two wildly different expressions met up in America and fused themselves into a uniquely American way of dancing. Black slaves had brought their dances, their songs, their music from Africa to the New World. The drum was the voice that

spoke to them of their ancestry. In 1739 a group of South Carolina slaves, "with colors flying and drums beating," sought to escape their masters. They were captured. Within a year a law was passed banning the use of drums by slaves, since drums could be considered as "inciting to insurrection."

The black slaves lost their drums but not their ancestral rhythms. The beats, the messages of drums were transferred to clappers made of bone and . . . to the feet. When the slaves began to dance for the pleasure of white masters as well as for self-entertainment, they copied some of the styles and steps of white people. In the Caribbean they did their own versions, often satiric, of white social dances from the court of France or the ballrooms of London or New York. In the United States itself, they found a certain rhythmic rapport with immigrant Irishmen who had brought their clog dances with them to America. The cloggers became popular entertainers. The blacks, taking the technique of the clog but investing the beats and stamps with the rhythms of Africa, evolved a new form that was to delight audiences around the world—tap.

The tap dancer, like the flamenco performer, is basically an improviser. Thus looking at tap one wants to savor the personality and inventiveness of the individual. When Bill Robinson danced with tiny Shirley Temple in the movies, the gentle, happy relationship of adult and child could be heard as well as seen. Robinson, on his own, turned on more sophisticated rhythms. The Nicholas Brothers ran up walls or the proscenium arch of the theater or jumped off platforms and landed in splits on the floor. Peg Leg Bates, who had lost a leg, made a specialty out of dancing with his wooden leg. Sandman Sims scattered sand on the floor (as Fred Astaire did in one of his films) and tapped ever so softly, slid and turned in dances as soothing as lullabies.

Ballroom dance on ice—
Palais de Glace, John Curry
(with JoJo Starbuck in IceDancing).

A class in tap, Ron Daniels, instructor.

There are tap dances for white tie, top hat and tails (in black or white dress); others of rural character (reminding us of the clog dance) done in overalls; and with a single soloist or a precision line of girls, glitter and glitz, long legs and flashy costumes may be in order. Paul Draper has tapped to jazz, to Bach and, in a wonderfully satiric number, to a speech by Adolf Hitler! And way back in the 1840s, a freeborn black named William Henry Lane took the stage name of Juba (derived from an African dance, the *giouba*) and rose to stardom as the black star of an all-white company of minstrel performers. Often hailed as "the greatest of dancers," Juba won acclaim abroad as well as at home for the intricacy, speed and variety of his steps. He strongly influenced the course of tap-dance techniques to come. Sounds as well as sight attracted audiences to Juba, for they not only looked, they listened. In a contest with a white dancer in blackface, Master Diamond, judges both observed and listened, for some sat out front and watched while others took their places beneath the stage to concentrate on the rhythms and intricacies of the steps. Juba, of course, won most of the contests in which he participated.

At dancing school, children not only learn to tap, usually as single

Star tap soloist—Peter Gennaro.

performers, but they also may take lessons in how to dance together. This, of course, is social (or ballroom) dancing. Attendance at such classes fluctuates with the times, because during the 1950s and 1960s, the couple dance, or "contact" dance, nearly disappeared as each dancer did his own thing on the ballroom floor. With the return of couple dances, instruction is helpful. The youngsters learn how to lead, follow or simply move together in harmony.

The foxtrot, the waltz and other social dances, including those of Latin American origin, are basics in ballroom dancing and are still done no matter what current fads take over for brief periods. This sort of dancing is recreational, and it is meant to be done—it is not a spectator sport. But early in this century a couple named Vernon and Irene Castle took the social dances of the day and by dancing them (with various elaborations) better than the average young couple or husband and wife, they came up with a new form of dance entertainment that was to be called "exhibition ballroom dancing." Vernon Castle was killed in World War I in a flying accident at an air base, but he and his wife had already changed American dance with the Castle Walk, the Bunny Hug, the Turkey Trot and a variety of social dances that became the rage of every dining and dancing spot in the land.

Almost everybody could copy the Castles well enough to enjoy doing, in simplified form, the Castle dances. During this World War I period, there were exhibition dancers who demonstrated and taught the Argentine tango at "tango teas." Ted Shawn, before he became the influential molder and star of a contemporary art dance form, earned money to pay for his concerts by dancing with a partner at tango teas.

In later years exhibition-ballroom-dance teams extended their range, showing not only popular steps of new dances, but augment-

ing them with balletic lifts and fast spins, swooping backbends and even splits. There were also teams who engaged in acrobatics, combining the skills of the gymnast-acrobat with the polish of the dancer. After World War I a very young Fred Astaire and his sister, Adele, rose to stardom in Broadway shows by doing specialty dances that used their tap-dance skills. Later, in Hollywood, with Ginger Rogers as his partner, Astaire combined tap and ballroom dancing in a way that retained the universal appeal of social dancing while exploiting the technique of a tap specialist.

While watching exhibition ballroom dances of this sort on the stage, in clubs, at the movies, the viewer can say to himself, "Oh, I can dance like that . . . well, almost . . . except for the taps." And, indeed Astaire and Rogers were, as were the Castles before them and others after them, simply you and me—social dancers, glorified.

In the field of entertainment, if the tap dancer is an exponent of a personal style, the eccentric dancer is even more personal, often unique. The eccentric dancer is just what the title promises. The viewer looks for the eccentricity as a novel experience. Gil Lamb, a variety dancer, had a body seemingly made of rubber; Charlotte Greenwood's long legs not only permitted her to kick way above her

Staying limber—Donna Wood.

Acrobatics in modern dance—Stephanie Baxter,
Mel Tomlinson in *Adagietto No. 5* (Dance Theatre of Harlem).

Gymnastics in dance—Pilobolus
in *Monkshood's Farewell*.

head, but also, in the middle of a routine, to walk over chairs, sofas and small automobiles. Hurricane Betsy combines flexibility with speed and, gifted as an artist, she executes a life-sized sketch on stage of the character she is going to portray in her next number.

Certain eccentricities of body, of costume or props are part of the eccentric dancer's material for variety shows. Gloria Gilbert, ballet-trained, had toe shoes with ball bearings installed so that she could do an incredible sequence of *pirouettes* from a single push-off. A contortionist dancer specialized in being the serpent in the Garden of Eden and spent most of the act slithering up and down the trunk

Adagio on ice—John Curry and Cathy Foulkes.

Dance virtuosity on ice—John Curry and Cathy Foulkes.

A mix of dance talent—ballet dancers Baryshnikov and Nureyev
partner Broadway jazz dancer Gwen Verdon in modern dancer
Paul Taylor's *From Sea to Shining Sea.*

and branches of an artificial tree. Some female dancers have put taps
on their toe shoes in order to do something called toe-tap—one of
them learned to play a cornet while toe-tapping. But way back in the
1790s, Alexander Placide came all the way from Paris to entertain
audiences in New York, Philadelphia and Charleston with his
balletic hornpipe on a tightrope, during which he "played the violin
while displaying the American flag in various attitudes." And about
five thousand years ago, Ethiopian dancing girls were imported to
Egypt to amuse Pharaoh with acrobatic dances that included
backbends resembling miniature arched bridges. Today's acrobatic

Another mix of dance talent: ballet's Rudolf Nureyev as the Preacher in Martha Graham's modern-dance masterpiece *Appalachian Spring* with William Carter, dancer of ballet, modern, and Spanish forms.

American religious folk ceremony theatricalized by the late Doris Humphrey in *The Shakers* (José Limón Dance Company) with Jennifer Scanlon as the Elderess.

160

American religious folk ceremony theatricalized by the late Doris Humphrey in *The Shakers* (José Limón Dance Company) with Jennifer Scanlon as the Elderess.

dancers know exactly what is meant by "bridge."

Precision is what we look for when it comes to mass uniform dancing such as the Rockettes are famous for. The individual Rockette does not do tap that would rival Eleanor Powell nor does she kick as high as Charlotte Greenwood—perhaps she can, but as a Rockette she is not required to be highly individual. On the contrary, she is expected to be almost anonymous. What is important here is that the thirty-six Rockettes tap, kick, turn, dip, bend, kneel in flawless unison, a living machine that is thrilling, and diverting, to watch. The dancing skaters in a big ice extravaganza must achieve that same precision but with the added peril of skates, ice and speed. The star skaters have time for their specialties, and the audience savors the particular tricks, graces, rhythms or virtuosities of individual stars, but for the company only precision matters.

A great skater like John Curry can go from winning Olympic and world skating titles as a sportsman to being a highly paid exhibition skater to assuming his unique role as the greatest dancer on skates in his new art form, *IceDancing*. A skater who zooms across the ice and vaults over a lineup of barrels has an enormously exciting and entertaining *act*. When Curry skates to Debussy's "The Afternoon of a Faun," originally composed for the great ballet dancer Vaslav Nijinsky, you are in the presence of a work of *art*. Both performances are valid, both entertaining, but their purposes are quite different and the response of the viewer varies accordingly.

Everyone responds happily as Ethel Merman belts out one of the great songs with which she is identified, "There's No Business Like Show Business," and all of us feel grateful to the performer symbolized in the song "Let Me Entertain You," but the greatest joy experienced by the viewer is when he knows that he can be entertained by a fine performance of Shakespeare's *Romeo and Juliet* as well as by the *Star Wars* movie; by Puccini's *La Bohème* as well as by a rock concert in the park; by Martha Graham's modern dance *Appalachian Spring* as well as by "Misha" dancing, singing and clowning with Liza Minnelli in the TV special *Baryshnikov on Broadway*.

VARIETY! What a wonderful word it is. Performing artists of every kind and cut provide audiences with an incredible variety of talents. All they ask in return is that we look at what they do with a like variety of responses. And with dance, one should look not only with one's eyes, but also with a body that responds, empathically or kinesthetically, with what the dancer is doing. The viewer, of course, is as important as the doer. Together they *are* DANCE.

9 The Meanings of

Various productions of Limón's *The Moor's Pavane* (Shakespeare's *Othello* in modern-dance form): Clay Taliafarro as the Moor, Carla Maxwell as Amelia, Jennifer Scanlon as Desdemona, Robert Swinston as Iago.

Movement

Every little movement has a meaning all its own,
Every thought and feeling by some posture may be shown.

These words were on almost everyone's lips in America seventy years ago. They were not the rhymed views of a François Delsarte or a revelation by Sigmund Freud; they were the opening lyrics in the hit tune written by Otto Harbach in 1910 for the musical, *Madame Sherry*. For the thousands who sang the song or hummed the tune, the words conjured up such simple and romantic acts as flirting, beckoning, pouting or, best of all, a kiss or an embrace. To Ted Shawn, who came upon the song long after the show had been forgotten while the melody (and words) lingered on, these lines represented, fortuitously, a popular equivalent of what Delsarte, the scientist of meaningful movement, had been trying desperately to get across to performers on stage. Shawn therefore in writing his enormously valuable book on Delsarte and his influence on dance called his work *Every Little Movement* (published in 1954).

Meaning is present in every movement from the flutter of an eyelid to a space-splitting leap. Yet in order to see and savor all that is present in a performance, we must bring something of ourselves to the occasion. (In English, we say that we "go to" the theater or "attend" a performance. The French have a much better expression, *assister*, "to assist.") Even though the theatergoer or attendant at a performance is held to a seat, that viewer must truly "assist" in a performance by looking for the choreographer's meanings, responding to the dancers' interpretations of the choreographer's intentions and bringing his or her own personal experiences or reactions to bear upon what is taking place on stage.

The job and the joy of "assisting" at a performance require some guidelines. Suppose you are in a dance studio watching a teacher instruct a student. At first, steps are taught—it doesn't matter whether it is the tap dancer's time step, the Spanish dancer's heel beat or the ballet dancer's *glissade*. Watch a little longer, and you will find the teacher telling the pupil where the arms should be, how the head is held, where the hips are placed and, indeed, what is to be done with every part of the anatomy at a given moment. The novice dancer will have to readjust everything for the count of two, again for the count of three (or for each musical half, quarter, eighth, and so on). But

Various productions of Limón's *The Moor's Pavane* (Shakespeare's *Othello* in modern-dance form): Clay Taliafarro as the Moor,

Carla Maxwell as Amelia, Jennifer Scanlon as Desdemona,
Robert Swinston as Iago.

Nureyev as the Moor,
Dame Margot Fonteyn as Desdemona.

this is merely technique, the raw material of dance. It isn't quite yet dance, at least not on a performing level.

Later, if you continue to watch the progress of the student, you will note that the teacher or coach may not mention steps at all or even technique. You will hear, instead, instructions in breathing, musical phrasing, dramatic timing, levels of energy to be expended, facial expression, and a hundred other details that will culminate in a full portrait in dance.

As for us, when we look at the final performance, we too must have our senses trained to respond to every detail of dance, from excellence of technique through command of style to those subtle nuances that give zest and flavor to a performance.

Probably one of the easiest dance forms to look at knowledgeably is the story ballet. There are whole scenes that are pantomimic, and since pantomime is the straightforward translation of thoughts, words and behavior into movement, the onlooker is contacted immediately and directly by the performers. In *Giselle,* for example, when a ruling Prince confronts the hero, Albrecht, who, though a count, is disguised as a peasant, the Prince makes a gesture that indicates curiosity about Albrecht's less than noble apparel. In pantomime he says, "Why, for heaven's sake, are you dressed like that?" Albrecht, replying in gesture, draws an imaginary bowstring as if to stay, "Oh, I've been out hunting with my bow and arrow." And interpretations of classical roles vary to some extent. Another dancer playing Albrecht might not use the bow-and-arrow gesture at all, but instead might shrug his shoulders and wave a hand casually by his head as if to say, "I know it looks crazy, but I was just out for a little fun." Either gesture is simple enough to understand, but what is important is that the difference in the gesture provides a clue as to how the dancer conceives the role of Albrecht: a nobleman who may possibly love Giselle, the peasant girl, but who must lie his way out of an awkward situation, or a nobleman who is simply dallying with a pretty lass.

Most pantomime in such ballets as *Giselle* or *Swan Lake* is fairly literal. But such old classics also include traditional gestures found in all ballets. Some are immediately understandable, while others take a bit of homework. For example, when Giselle points to her ring finger, it is apparent that she is telling someone she is engaged to be married. When the Princess-Mother in *Swan Lake* points to her son and then to the ring finger, it is pretty clear that she is telling him the time has come for him to marry. Other gestures are less specific. Arms folded across the breast usually refer to a mother; arms crossed at the wrists and held low in front of the body signify doom or death, and arms raised with clenched fists denote evil or the villain himself.

In a scene like that in *Swan Lake* when Odette, the Swan Queen, tells the Prince (whom she has just met) how she became a swan, it is therefore possible to follow an explanation based on a combination of specific and symbolic gestures. In this way we discover that she is held in the thrall of an evil magician, that the lake of swans we see in the background is made of her mother's tears, that she will be released from the spell only if a nobleman asks her to marry him and swears on his honor to love no other. The ensuing tragedy of *Swan Lake* is that the malevolent magician substitutes his evil daughter, Odile, for Odette, and the Prince, inadvertently breaking his vow to Odette by pledging marriage to Odile disguised as Odette, brings doom to all. If the balletgoer follows Odette's mimed narrative in Act II, everything that happens in Acts III and IV takes on new urgency, suspense and excitement.

Modern dance is something else again. In José Limón's *The Moor's Pavane,* it is clear when Iago puts his head close to Othello's

Nureyev as the Moor,
Louis Falco as Iago.

170

and whispers in his ear that something is being said. Othello's reaction, with head thrust forward and shoulders tensed, tells the audience that the Moor is angry and disbelieving. But as Iago continues to plant his lies about Desdemona, he wraps a leg around Othello, and through explicit pantomime extended into a symbolic movement, we know that Othello has been caught in Iago's toils, enmeshed in his falseness. Shakespeare's words are not present to unfold the tale, but choreographed movement is present to lead us deep into the bodies and, thence, into the passions of the dancers.

The dances of India make use of a different sort of pantomime. Certain gestures represent a bounding deer, a vain peacock, a lumbering elephant, or perhaps a hovering bird ready to carry love's message. These gestures are both pictorial and meaningful. And there are others, equally fetching to the eye, that possess information or meaning but which are so symbolic in form that they require explanation. One movement in this category would be *sundari,* the gliding neck shift, which serves rather like an exclamation point at the end of a sentence in movement. Palms pressed together express, in many cultures, prayer or prayerful attitudes. In Indian dance the gesture serves in several capacities as, say, an invocation, an obeisance, a benediction. The dancer salutes the audience with palms together and a bow. Its meaning? Ruth St. Denis preferred one above others: "I salute the god that lies within you."

In addition to pantomimic movements and symbolic (or ritualized) movements, the ethnic dancer, the modern dancer, the ballet dancer—any sort of dancer—often deals with movements that contain no explicit meanings whatsoever. These can be thought of as "abstract" or nonliteral. A beautiful design, geometric or asymmetric; the thrust of a muscled male body into space; the suspension of a female body on *pointe;* a cascade of foot beats, Spanish or tap; a pattern of raised arms may have meanings that are no more literal than sunlight, moonlight, starlight or twilight, yet all are real, all have significance, and none requires explanation.

Choreographers not only make use of traditional gestures and movements, but also make up new movements or new arrangements of familiar movements to express individual ideas in individual ways. When Antony Tudor created *Shadowplay,* a ballet reminiscent of Rudyard Kipling's *Kim,* he devised for his boy hero a semisitting position suggesting an invisible throne. It was not the squat of an animal, for the pose was elegant, with one arm resting lightly on an extended knee as if the knee were the arm of the throne. The posture was erect, for here was a boy king; and the half-crouch, half-sitting position indicated the alertness of a jungle creature. Thus, through an invented pose, the choreographer made us see a situation, a person, that person's rank, that individual's special characteristics and, even more, the anticipatory nature of the character and his environment.

The signature work for the Alvin Ailey American Dance Theater is Ailey's glorious and exuberant *Revelations*. It incorporates modern dance, folk dance, social dance and freely invented action deriving from black American heritage, especially as expressed through Negro spirituals. Audiences respond to the full-company finale, "Rocka My Soul in the Bosom of Abraham" with shouts, cheers and rhythmic clappings as if they too were participants in a great revival meeting. Earlier, for the spiritual "Fix Me, Jesus," Ailey conceived a duet of supplication for a man and a woman. It is reverent yet quietly ecstatic, and the key gesture is a reach toward the invisible Jesus. The culmination of this motif of reaching is achieved at the final moment, when the woman steps on her partner's thigh and with her entire body—not merely her hand and arm—reaches heavenward. Dance moments such as these demand, or at least invite, a kinesthetic response from the viewer.

Kinesthetics is not nearly as frightening as it sounds. In brief, it means that you not only *look* at dance but you respond to it with your own body. If the eye can retain an image of something seen and the ear capture and recall a melody, so can the viewer of a dance event receive in his or her own muscles echoes of action. We experience this body awareness every day of our lives, although not necessarily aesthetically. For instance, you see someone slip on an icy pavement. Instinctively you react with a movement of trying to save yourself from falling, although you are quite safe. Such ordinary kinetic response is called empathy, a movement equivalent to sympathy.

If empathy is developed aesthetically, it becomes kinesthetics. A child's responses are quite uninhibited. Children, at the circus or at the ballet, will jump up and down, peek through their fingers when aerialists zoom through death-defying flights and spin in the aisles in imitation of pirouettes. As children, their kinesthetic responses are permitted to be overt. Adults are not granted such freedom—their responses must be contained as they experience the sensations of

motion within themselves.

Children, then, have natural instincts requiring no tutoring in order to express their feelings. But even they must go beyond instinct. Their formal education begins with exposure to and training in an elementary course of study that American folkways long ago designated The Three R's: *readin', 'ritin'* and *'rithmetic.* How far the child went depended not only on parental pressure but on individual goals.

Kinesthetics in the individual can be developed similarly to minimal or maximum degrees. The choice is up to the one who

Nureyev as the Moor,
Winthrop Corey as Iago,
Mary Jago as Desdemona,
Linda Maybarduk as Amelia.

looks at dance and determines how much or how little he or she wishes to see. The newcomer to dance might well find a dance equivalent of the traditional three R's helpful. Obviously, one could use S's or T's or some other commonly used letter of the English alphabet, but the R's, with their traditional familiarity, are acceptable. But let us call them the R's of Dramatic Movement. Student dancers are but dimly aware of the power inherent in these R's; young dancers exploit a few; the great dancers make use of all of them.

The dancer's body at REST is not in itself very exciting, but it has

The position for the Jungle Boy in Tudor's
Shadowplay (rehearsal, George de la Peña).

value as a contrast to action, as a pause in the midst of action, or as a prelude to action. As the body moves into position for ballet, modern, tap—or for any form of dance expression—the dancer moves from REST to READY. (This happens with the jungle boy in *Shadowplay*. The subtle change is illustrated in two accompanying photographs.) The next moment comes when the dancer REALIZES— and makes us, the audience, REALIZE—who he is, where he is and what the situation may be. As the music dictates or invites, or as the story in dance unfolds, the dancer will be required to invest movements with meanings that indicate a state of affairs that exists at the very moment of our looking. This dramatic state (or mood) may be inimical, angry or romantic, highly charged or gently yielding. Thus, from REST to READY to REALIZE, the dancer may REACH or REPEL, RESIST or RETALIATE, or the dancer might take us from carefree REVEL to ecstatic REJOICE.

These R's of dramatic movement, though varied in meaning and in mood, are all outgoing, positive actions. But suppose ominous music or the demands of plot lead the performer in a different direction. From REST the sequence might drift, stagger or plunge backward along a different path through REFUSE, REJECT, RECOIL, RETREAT, RETIRE. These provide guideposts to tragedy. But all is not lost! There are options: RECONSIDER, RECOVER, REGROUP, RECOUP.

These and other major R's of dramatic dance—the viewer may add many more if desired, as a sort of game of RECOGNITION—are shown in these pages in chart form accompanied by illustrative photographs. These lists of R's make no pretense of being laws of gesture—there never should be such laws governing the creation of and response to art expressions—but they may serve as guidelines just as a cardiogram serves as an indicator to doctor and patient of the physical functioning of the heart.

Baryshnikov as the Jungle Boy
(with Vladimir Gelvan) in *Shadowplay*.

For the romantic or dramatic function of the heart, considering the heart in a symbolic sense, Delsarte used thermometers, measurers of body heat. He used the word, of course, in a symbolic sense as he "took the temperature" of emotions through the movements of shoulders, elbows, wrists. (He considered legs "the beast of burden," less expressive than the arms.)

Cardiograms and thermometers are simply indicators not only of a state of being but of what further to anticipate. Our R's, for both dancer and viewer, are just that, no more. So for those who truly wish to *assister* at a performance, do not REFRAIN from participating

178

in the dance movements you watch in the theater or on television. REACH out with all your kinesthetic powers at the READY toward the dance in all its forms, and you will discover that you have cause to REJOICE.

Isadora Duncan, great performer that she was, also RELISHED looking at the dance. Watching her little niece run and skip and turn and leap on the sand by the sea, she said, "To her it is a joy to dance; to me it is a joy to watch her." Havelock Ellis, the English philosopher, put it more seriously: "If we are indifferent to the art of dancing, we have failed to understand, not merely the supreme manifestation of physical life, but also the supreme symbol of spiritual life."

And for all those who have learned to look at dance in order that they may see it from its tiniest, jewel-like details to its many splendors, Lord Byron, the poet, said it all in a rousing command: "ON WITH THE DANCE! LET JOY BE UNCONFINED."

THE 3 "R'S" *REVERBERATING* IN DANCE
Gestural REactions
(See following pages of illustrations)

R E S T

Ready
(alerted)

Relax

Realize

REceive

Refuse

Reach

REconsider

Relent

Resist

REconcile

Regret

Return

REcover

Reject

Rebound

REgroup

Refrain
(hold back)

Regain

REcoup

Retaliate

Retire

Repel

Recoil

Revel

Retreat

Relish

Rejoice

The "R's" (Positive)

Rest—Paul Taylor Dance Co.

Rest—Lowell Smith, Dance
Theatre of Harlem

Ready—
Rudolf Nureyev,
Margot Fonteyn

Ready—
George de la Peña

Ready—Paul Taylor Dance Co.

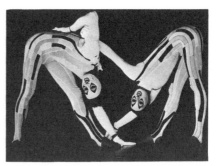

Ready—Nikolais Dance Theatre

Receive—George de la Peña   Realize—Cynthia Gregory, Erik Bruhn

Reach—
Rebecca Wright

Reach—
Peggy Lyman

183

Reach—Rebecca Wright, George de la Peña

Reach—Dudley Williams

Reach—Cynthia Gregory, Ivan Nagy

Reach—Rudolf Nureyev

Reach—Lane Sayles

Reach—Jorge Donn

184

Reach (opposing)—Lee Provancha Day, John Hiatt

Resist—Christopher Gillis, Carolyn Adams

Recover—
Paul Taylor Dance Co.

Rebound—Linda Kent,
Christopher Gillis

Rebound—Richard Cragun,
Charles Ward, Richard Schafer

Regain—
Paul Taylor Dance Co.

Regain—
Jorge Donn, Daniel Lommel

186

Retaliate—Lowell Smith

Retaliate—
Jorge Donn

Repel—Carla Fracci,
Mikhail Baryshnikov

187

Revel—Carmen de Lavallade

Revere—Barton Mumaw

Revel—Lazaro Carreño,
Maria Elena Llorente

Relish—Cynthia Gregory,
Rudolf Nureyev

Rejoice—Louis Falco
Dance Co.

Rejoice—Donna Wood,
Maxine Sherman

The "R's" (Negative)

Relax—Paul Taylor Dance Co.

Relax—Joffrey Ballet

Regret—Rudolf Nureyev,
Margot Fonteyn

Reject—Rudolf Nureyev

Reject—Elisa Monte,
George White, Jr.

Reject—Lydia Abarca, Ronald Perry

Retire—
Ailey Co.

Retire—Nadezhda
Pavlova, Vyacheslav
Gordeyev

Recoil—George de la Peña

Recoil—Rebecca Wright

Retreat—Jorge Donn

Retreat—Ailey Co.

Glossary of Dance Terms

BALLET

ADAGIO A dance in slow tempo. Also, that portion of a classical *pas de deux* in which the *ballerina,* assisted by her partner, displays her beauty of line and her mastery of flowing, lyrical and sustained movements.

Adagio (classical)—Odette, *Swan Lake*—Rebecca Wright, George de la Peña

Adagio (neoclassical)—Rebecca Wright, George de la Peña, *Prodigal Son*

ALLEGRO A dance sequence in fast tempo.

ARABESQUE A traditional ballet position in which the dancer stands on one leg
with the other leg extended behind in a straight line. Positions of the arms may
vary. In an *arabesque penché,* for example, the body is tilted forward and the
free leg extends high into space, sometimes reaching a position vertical to the
floor.

Arabesque (on
ice)—John Curry,
*Afternoon of a
Faun*

Arabesque—Stephanie Dabney

Arabesque—
Marcia Haydée,
Richard Cragun

Arabesque—
Rebecca Wright,
George de la Peña

Arabesque (supported)
—Cynthia Gregory,
Jonas Kage, *Gemini*

196

ATTITUDE A traditional ballet position in which the dancer stands on one leg with the other leg raised behind the body but with bent knee. The pose was inspired by Bologna's famed statue of the god Mercury. If the free leg is extended to the front, instead of the rear, and adheres to the same spatial design as the movement described above, it may also be referred to as an *attitude*.

Attitude—Claude de Vulpian, Patrick Dupond

Attitude—Fernando Bujones

Attitude—Rebecca Wright,
George de la Peña

Attitude (supported)—Frank Augustyn,
Karen Kain, *La Fille Mal Gardée*

BALLERINA The term is misused when applied to any female dancer. The *ballerina* is a leading female dancer in a ballet company, and if a major company has two or more *ballerinas* on its roster of stars, the principal one may be called a *prima ballerina*. The highest rank, given to the greatest female dancer of a nation and of an era, is *prima ballerina assoluta*.

BALLET Derived from the Italian word *ballare,* meaning "to dance."

BALLET D'ACTION A ballet with a story.

BALLETOMANE A person devoted to the ballet, a fan, who attends as many performances as possible, is an appreciative and critical viewer and strives to interest others in the art.

BALLON A term applicable to the execution of all dance movements in air. The resilience of the dancer and his ability to rise easily off the ground in a jump or leap and to descend lightly.

BARRE The pole (usually of wood) placed horizontally (attached to the walls) around a ballet studio as a support for the dancer in initial exercises.

BATTEMENT A kick, either high *(grand battement)* or low. In a *battement tendu,* the kick extends only as far as the stretched foot will allow with the tip of the toe remaining on the floor. It may be done in any direction.

Battement—Nadezhda Pavlova, *Spartacus* (Bolshoi Ballet)

Battement (jazz)—Marianna Tcherkassky, Mikhail Baryshnikov, Martine van Hamel

Battement—Rudolf Nureyev

Dégagé or battement—Cynthia Gregory, *Grand Pas Classique* (American Ballet Theatre)

BATTERIE The term applied to all movements in which the legs and feet beat together, usually in air *(entrechat, brisé, cabriole,* etc.). In the classroom certain preparatory exercises involving beats are done at the ballet *barre.* The dancer stands on one foot while the free foot accomplishes the beats.

198

BOURRÉE See *PAS DE BOURRÉE.*

BRISÉ A leg beat in the air. The dancer rises from the floor, beats one leg against the other and lands on both feet in *fifth position.* A *brisé* varies from the *entrechat* in that only one leg does the beating movement, and it varies from the *cabriole* in that the landing is made on both feet.

CABRIOLE A virtuosic movement in air (usually for male dancers but not exclusively) in which one leg swings out in a high kick and is held at the peak of its extension, while the other leg leaves the floor and strikes it in a swift beat or beats. The legs are straight, the feet pointed and the movement may be done to the front, rear or side. (The dancer lands on the foot that leaves the floor last.) See *BRISÉ.*

Cabriole—Rudolf Nureyev

Cabriole—
Alexander Godunov

CARACTÈRE A term used to describe a dancer who performs nonclassical character or national dances—such as *czardas* or a gypsy dance, in a ballet. A *demi-caractère* dancer is one who is called upon to combine character steps with classical action.

CHANGEMENT DE PIEDS A step in which the dancer jumps from *fifth position,* changes the feet in the air and lands in *fifth position* but with the position of the feet reversed (if the dancer starts with the right leg in front, he will finish with the right leg in back).

CHOREOGRAPHER The creator of a ballet, the one who invents, selects and designs the steps and the movements, and puts them into rhythmic, geometric or dramatic sequences that have form, progression and purpose.

CODA The concluding portion of a *pas de deux* or a ballet.

CORPS DE BALLET The chorus or ensemble of a ballet company.

CORYPHÉE A dancing rank that lies between the *corps de ballet* dancer and the soloist. One who is assigned a few phrases of movement distinct from the actions of the *corps* but who does not perform a complete solo.

199

Curtain call—
Alicia Alonso with
Jorge Esquivel,
White Swan

Curtain call—Rudolf
Nureyev

DANSE D'ÉCOLE The classic dance, the dance based upon the traditional technique of the classical ballet.

DANSEUR (Classical male dancer) *Premier danseur* is the first male dancer of a company.

DANSEUR NOBLE A classical male dancer distinguished by purity of classical style and elegance of bearing. Princely.

DÉVELOPPÉ The gradual unfolding of the leg as it is raised in an extension from the floor. Performed to the front, back or side. The unfolding action is centered in the knee, which bends as the working leg is withdrawn from the floor and which is straightened when the peak of the extension is concluded.

DIVERTISSEMENT A dance or a series of danced episodes without plot. An entire ballet may be a *divertissement,* or the term may apply to the "diverting" interludes in a dramatic ballet.

ÉCHAPPÉ A step in which the dancer's feet move swiftly from a "closed" to an "open" position, and from soles flat on the floor to *demi-pointe* or, in the case of the female dancer, full *pointe.* Executed from *first* or *fifth positions* to *second position,* either with a jump or with a quick *relevé.*

ELEVATION Aerial action, the ability of the dancer to move as easily in air as on the ground. (Related to the *ballon.*)

EN ARRIÈRE To the back.

EN AVANT To the front.

EN DEDANS Inward (toward the body).

EN DEHORS Outward (away from the body).

ENTRECHAT A vertical jump, with the body held in a plumb line, during which the dancer changes the position of his feet several times with a beating of the legs. The number of changes achieved indicate an *entrechat quatre, entrechat six,* etc.

ENTRÉE An entrance, such as the opening passages of a *grand pas de deux* or a suite of dances.

FIVE POSITIONS The traditional positions of the feet (there are related and numbered positions of the arms also) in ballet.

FOUETTÉ A whipping movement of the working leg which propels the dancer into a turn, into multiple turns of shifts of direction.

GLISSADE A smooth, gliding movement starting from *fifth position,* separating into a open-leg position (rather like a leap held to the floor) and returning to *fifth position.*

JETÉ A leap in which the dancer pushes off the floor with one leg, describes an arc in air and lands on the other foot. In a *grand jeté,* the dancer seeks the highest elevation possible, with the leading leg thrusting out and up as high as the body structure will permit and the propelling leg, once it has left the floor, reaching back to a high extension. Sometimes a near split may be achieved in a *grand jeté.*

Grand jeté (modern leap)—
Mel Tomlinson

Jeté (character)—
Jorge Donn

LEOTARD A body-fitting, one-piece garment resembling a bathing suit.

LIBRETTO The story of a ballet, or the plot, incident or theme on which it is based.

Lift—George de la Peña, Rebecca Wright, *Interplay*

NOTATION A script method for writing down the movements of a dance or ballet so that they may be revived or reproduced by others capable of reading the script. Methods employing stick figures, sometimes placed on a musical staff and in other cases paired with musical symbols, have been used for several centuries. The most exact form of notation known today is called *Labanotation*. Another contemporary notational method, developed in England, is the *Benesh system*.

PANTOMIME Imitative movement, usually gestural, by which emotions, character and the key points in a plot are communicated to an audience. Both realistic and stylized gestures may be used. Among the traditional ones used in ballet, those indicating Love (the hands are pressed against the heart) or Anger (arms are raised above the head and fists are shaken) can be considered reasonably realistic, while Dance (hands circling around each other over the head) and Queen (the index finger touches either side of the brow where a crown might rest) would be looked upon as stylized gestures.

PAS A danced step or movement. Also used to denote a short dance or dance passage (in this sense, usually used with a modifier, such as *pas seul* or *pas de deux,* etc.).

PAS D'ACTION Episodes in ballet that advance the plot, introduce dramatic incident or establish relationships among the characters. A combination of dancing and pantomime.

PAS DE BASQUE A light, sliding step (the name derives from Basque dancing).

PAS DE BOURRÉE A walking step, usually swift, done on the ball of the foot or, with the female dancer, on *pointe*. The dancer may travel in any direction, and the steps are customarily so short that the separation between the dancer's legs as she or he moves is barely discernible.

PAS DE CHAT A catlike step. From a *plié* in *fifth position,* the dancer leaps into the air, drawing up one leg (with bent knee) and immediately duplicating the action with the other leg so that at the peak of elevation, the toes almost meet in air.

PAS DE DEUX A dance for two. A classical *grand pas de deux* is performed by a *ballerina* and a *premier danseur* and is divided into *entrée, adagio,* two *variations* and *coda.* Also, *pas de trois* (a dance for three), *pas de quatre* (for four), *pas de cinq* (for five), *pas de six* (for six), etc.

PAS DE POISSON A climactic movement in a phrase of action in which the female dancer hurls herself headfirst in the direction of the floor and is caught by her partner as her body bends upward in a fishlike arc. When the male dancer jumps upward and describes a similar arc of the body, the movement may also be described as a *pas de poisson,* although this male movement is actually a form of *soubresaut.* The same body line is described in space at the peak of a *carbriole en arrière.*

PIROUETTE A turn of the body on one foot. Usually the female does the movement on *pointe,* the male, always on *demi-pointe* (on the ball of the foot). The free leg may be held in any number of approved positions against the ankle of the working leg or higher up along the calf, straight out to the side (*à la seconde, en attitude,* etc.).

PLIÉ A bending of the knees, with the hips, legs and feet turned outward. A *demi-*

plié is a small knee bend, while a *grand plié* is a deep knee bend. This is the movement that enables the dancer to spring up high into the air and to return to the ground (when a second plié is done) lightly, without jarring.

POINTE The tip of the toe. The female dancer, when she is dancing *sur les pointes* (or, more popularly, on *pointe*), is moving on the tips of her toes and wearing blocked toe slippers, which give her added support. Toe dancing, incidentally, is not synonymous with the word *ballet,* for ballet existed long before the *ballerina* rose onto *pointe* and long before the toe shoe was invented. *Pointe* dancing added new physical peril, new movement possibilities and new beauty to the basic, established technique of ballet.

PORT DE BRAS The positions and the movements of the arms.

Port de bras (character)—
Victoria Uris, *Images*

Lift—Sean Lavery, Suzanne Farrell,
Romeo and Juliet

RELEVÉ Rising onto *pointe* or *demi-pointe.*

RÉVÉRENCE A low, courtly, graceful bow.

ROND DE JAMBE A rotary movement of the leg either on the floor or in the air.

SAUTÉ A jump.

TERRE-À-TERRE Steps that are done on the ground.

TIGHTS The skintight garment that encases the body from trunk to feet.

TOUR A turn. A *pirouette* is a *tour,* but the term is usually employed with a modifier, such as *tour jeté, tour en l'air,* etc.

TOUR EN L'AIR One of the most brilliant movements for the male dancer (although it is sometimes executed by the female). From *fifth position* in *demi-plié,* the dancer springs straight up into the air and does a complete turn of the body before landing in the position from which he started. Most male dancers can accomplish a double turn in air, a few can do triples. In a virtuosic sequence the male dancer may be called upon to execute a whole series of doubles, one right after the other.

TURNOUT The body position characteristic of ballet, with the legs turned out from the hips at a 90-degree angle for each side (with professional dancers and advanced students but *not* beginners).

TUTU The skirt worn by the female ballet dancer. In the romantic style (instituted by Taglioni), it reached almost to the ankle. In the later classic style it has been shortened so the entire leg is revealed, the *tutu* extending out from the hips rather like a huge powder puff.

VARIATION A solo dance. The same as *pas seul*.

TAP

BRUSH Touching the floor with the tap as it goes forward.

CRAMP ROLL A sound made by placing the ball of one foot on the floor, then the other one, then dropping the heel of the first and that of the second.

DRAG Stepping back on one foot, then sliding the other foot to meet it.

FLAP Same as a SLAP.

HOP Literally hopping on the ball of either foot.

PULLBACK Spanking one foot while the other foot is off the floor, then landing on the ball of the foot just spanked.

SCUFF Sound of the heel tap hitting the floor while moving forward.

SHUFFLE A double sound made by brushing the front tap forward, then back. Can also be done to the side by brushing out, then in.

SLAP Brushing the foot forward, then stepping on the ball of that foot.

SPANK Sound made when brushing backward.

STAMP Sound of whole foot placed on the floor.

STEP A single sound made by placing the foot on the floor.

TAP Hitting the floor with the ball of the foot and lifting it while weight is on the other foot.

TOE-TAP Four sounds made by going up on one toe, then the other, then returning to the floor.

WING A step consisting of three sounds done by one foot. The foot brushes to the side, then brushes in and finishes on the ball of the foot.

JAZZ DANCE

(There is no standard terminology for jazz dance, for jazz dance is rooted in an individual response to jazz rhythms. Its base can be the adapted techniques of ballet, modern dance, social dance, tap and even ethnic forms. The glossary on Tap includes steps used with jazz rhythms. This glossary lists a few examples of jazz, social and/or ballroom dances of various periods.)

Jazz (character)—Mikhail Baryshnikov   Jazz—Jorge Donn

BIG APPLE A group dance, using a folk-dance circle form but with a jazz beat in the execution of steps.

BOOGIE-WOOGIE A jazz music style (with eight beats to the bar and a ruffled bass) primarily for piano, but becoming popular as accompaniment for social dance in the 1930s.

CAKEWALK Prejazz dance of African ancestry, with minstrel origins, and characterized by prancing steps, front kicks and a leaning back of the body, done in circles or a line in the form of a promenade.

CHA-CHA-CHA Cuban dance using two slow and three quick steps.

CHARLESTON The rage of the 1920s. A frenetic dance featuring turned-in knees, from which low kicks to the side and back are executed; kicks crossing diagonally in front of the body and toward the back; spreading and closing knees as hands on kneecaps shift back and forth; and other step patterns.

CONGA Afro-Cuban chain dance in which each dancer places hands on hips of dancer in front. The dance, in 4/4 time, has a pattern of three steps and a low kick. The number of participants can be few or many and the space covered, a ballroom or an entire town.

FOXTROT An enduring ballroom dance spanning ragtime and jazz. In 4/4 time, it is a jazzier version of the two-step (two quicks and a slow) through breaking up the rhythms into other components.

JITTERBUG Dance in swingtime in the 1930s allowing for individual improvisation of steps.

LINDY A jitterbug dance for couples that not only involves fast steps of the basic jitterbug, but also elaborate, improvised acrobatics, which include the male partner flipping his female partner over his head, around his waist, in slides between his legs, etc.

205

MAMBO A 1950s Cuban dance—a mix of Latin and jazz rhythms.

MAXIXE Originating in Brazil, it became an American and European ballroom dance favorite with its sensuous style and Latin flavor.

ROCK DANCES Almost always solo dances, done in the 1960s when couple dancing nearly disappeared. Among many, these included the TWIST (associated mainly with Chubby Checker), the FRUG, the HULLY-GULLY. With the 1970s, ROCK for couples came in with the HUSTLE as the most popular of these dances.

SHIMMY A solo jazz dance of the 1920s involving the shaking of hips at rapid speed and related undulations.

TANGO From the Argentine, an international favorite because of its call for close embraces, slinkiness of step and Latin airs. So popular during World War I, most hotels in U.S. cities featured "Tango Teas."

MODERN DANCE

Modern dance, unlike ballet, has no traditional vocabulary of movement and no standard terminology. It developed concurrently in the United States and Central Europe during this century, and each of its key originators and their successors expressed their principles in different ways. Thus, Martha Graham based her body-training techniques on the concept of CONTRACTION and RELEASE of the muscles. Doris Humphrey visualized her area of dance as lying between the gravity-pictured poles of FALL and RECOVERY. Charles Weidman focused on evolving KINETIC PANTOMIME, an instinctive, nonliteral gestural response to stimuli as distinct from the

Gymnastic—Pilobolus

206

Jump (character)—Jean Babilée, *Life*   Jump—Lila York, *Esplanade*

traditional mime of classical ballet or the literal pantomime of the *commedia dell'arte*.

German modern dance, as originated by Rudolf von Laban and Mary Wigman, created movement disciplines based upon the polar extremes of TENSION and RELAXATION and the degrees of expendable energy lying in between, a concept also described as *anspannung* and *abspannung* (the "inflow" and "outflow" of energy).

In modern dance, as well as in jazz dance and in certain forms of tap, ballet terms are frequently used by teachers in classrooms as shortcuts to anatomical explanations and descriptions, since ballet terminology is standard worldwide and since most professional dancers study ballet.

Lift (acrobatic)—Lowell Smith, Stephanie Dabney, *Manifestations*   Lift—Lowell Smith, Cassandra Phifer, *The Beloved*

ETHNIC DANCE

Ethnic dance represents the dances of a people, a nation, a culture, a region as distinct from dance forms developed by academies (such as ballet) or individuals (like modern dance). Ethnic dance includes (1) FOLK DANCE, social and communal dances that can be executed by everyone and are principally recreational, and (2) ETHNIC (or ETHNOLOGIC) ART DANCES requiring trained executants or performers (temple dancers, ritual dancers, theater dancers). Elaborate terminologies for movements, gestures, styles, schools exist for several of the world's major ETHNIC-ART-DANCE expressions, but since they are expressed in languages foreign to English-speaking readers, only a few examples are shown here with concentration on the DANCE OF INDIA and the DANCE OF SPAIN.

Spanish Dance:

BOLERO A Spanish classical dance of Moorish origin in ¾ time. It belongs in the category of "school dances" (dances learned through instruction) and possesses ballet characteristics.

CASTANETS Carved pieces of wood, with concave centers that meet when clapped, ruffled or rolled by the fingers to make percussion accompaniment for the dancers. The castanets fit into the palms of the hands. Originally used exclusively by Spanish gypsies; today used in other than flamenco dances. (In Spanish, *Castañuelas*.)

FLAMENCO A gypsy from Seville, and the style of dance originated by Spanish gypsies.

GITANO (GITANA) Gypsy.

JOTA A regional dance that is neither flamenco nor "school" and uses no *taconeo*. It contains jumps and other aerial action, and was, in antiquity, a fertility dance designed to encourage the growth of crops. The most popular of Spain's jotas is the JOTA ARAGONESA.

PALMADA Clapping.

PITO Finger snappings.

SEVILLANAS The Andalusian dance that is sometimes considered the national dance of Spain. In ⅜ (or ¾) time, it was once danced by one or two couples, but for the stage it can be done as a solo or with any number of dancers. It is a theme-and-variations kind of dance, intricate of step and aristocratic of stance.

TACONEO Heel work, foot rhythms made audible. Flamenco.

ZAPATEADO A dance featuring elaborate *taconeo* in a wide variety of rhythms, speeds and controlled loudnesses and softnesses of the stamping feet. Flamenco. Traditionally a man's dance, but today occasionally danced by women.

Indian Dance:

ANJALI The position of the hands when palms are pressed together in the gesture of prayer, supplication, invocation, etc.

BHARATA NATYAM The ancient classical dance of India with origins dating back two thousand years and more. Originally performed by highly skilled temple dancers. Until recently, a woman's dance. For contemporary theater, men may dance in this style.

KATHAK The popular dance school of northern India with strong Muslim influences. Some of the dances tell stories, but many are pure dance entertainment exploiting a variety of rhythms and moods.

KATHAKALI India's dance-drama telling in dance form such Hindu epics as the *Ramayana*. The actor-dancers are usually men. The costumes and masks painted on the faces in many colors are elaborate and often wildly grotesque. Pantomime, using hand gestures, facial expressions and body movements, is fused with rhythmic action.

MANIPURI A dance school of northern India presenting tales of local folklore through lyrical, sweeping movement.

MUDRAS (or *hasta-mudras*). The elaborate gesture language of the Hindu dance. Composed of a vocabulary of hand gestures of pictorial and symbolic meanings requiring great virtuosity on the part of the performer.

NATYA Dance with dramatic meaning.

NRITTA Pure dance.

NRITYA Dance that expresses sentiment.

SHIVA (or *Síva*). The member of the Hindu trinity of gods most closely associated with dance, especially in his guise of Nataraja, Lord of the Dance.

SUNDARI With the neck mobile and controlled, the head (upright) glides back and forth (or in a circle) across the shoulders. It has no literal meaning other than to punctuate a movement phrase, or to underscore the importance of a gestural statement.

Other Ethnic-Dance Art Examples:

JAPAN The *Noh* plays and the *Kabuki* dance-dramas.

INDONESIA *Wayang Wong,* Javanese dance-drama; *Legong* and *Kebiyar,* popular dances of Bali.

HAWAII The *hula* (meaning "dance"), the most famous of all Polynesian dances. Originally a "sitting" dance that told stories through gesture; later, a standing dance with hip movements added.

Suggested Reading

The Art of the Dance, Isadora Duncan. New York: Theater Art Books, 1960, reprint.

Ballet Guide, Walter Terry. New York: Dodd, Mead and Company, 1976. (Also available in paperback reprint, Popular Library, 1977.)

Black Dance in the United States from 1619 to 1970, Lynn Fauley Emery. New York: Dance Horizons, Inc., 1980, reprint.

The Book of Tap, Recovering America's Long Lost Dance, Jerry Ames and Jim Siegelman. New York: David McKay Company, Inc., 1977.

The Borzoi Book of Modern Dance, Margaret Lloyd. New York: Dance Horizons, Inc., reprint.

Classical Ballet: The Flow of Movement, Tamara Karsavina. New York: Dance Horizons, Inc., 1962, reprint.

The Concise Oxford Dictionary of Ballet, Horst Koegler. New York: Oxford University Press, 1977.

Dance, Jack Anderson. New York: Newsweek Books, 1979.

Dance, A Short History of Classic Theatrical Dancing, Lincoln Kirstein. New York: Dance Horizons, Inc., 1969, reprint.

The Dance in America, Walter Terry. New York: DaCapo Press, 1981, reprint.

The Dance in India, Faubion Bowers. New York: Columbia University Press, 1953.

Delsarte System of Expression, Genevieve Stebbins. New York: Dance Horizons, Inc., 1977, reprint.

Every Little Movement, Ted Shawn. New York: Dance Horizons, Inc., 1963, reprint.

Great Male Dancers of the Ballet, Walter Terry. Garden City, N.Y.: Anchor Books, 1978.

I Was There, Walter Terry. New York: Marcel Dekker, Inc., 1978.

Jazz Dance, the Story of American Vernacular Dance, Marshall and Jean Stearns. New York: Schirmer Books, 1968.

The King's Ballet Master, Walter Terry. New York: Dodd, Mead and Company, 1979.

Letters on Dancing and Ballets, Jean Georges Noverre. New York: Dance Horizons, Inc., 1966, reprint.

The Luigi Jazz Dance Technique, Kenneth Wydro. Garden City, N.Y.: Doubleday and Company, 1981.

On Mime, Angna Enters. Middletown, Conn.: Wesleyan University Press, 1965.

On Tap Dancing, Paul Draper. New York: Marcel Dekker, Inc., 1978.

Pre-classic Dance Forms, Louis Horst. New York: Dance Horizons, Inc., 1972, reprint.

Spanish Dancing, La Meri (Russell Meriwether Hughes). New York: A. S. Barnes, 1948.

The Thinking Body, Mabel Elsworth Todd. New York: Dance Horizons, Inc., 1968, reprint.

Total Education in Ethnic Dance, La Meri (Russell Meriwether Hughes). New York: Marcel Dekker, Inc., 1977.

Index